SHACKLED TO FREE!

GETTING GOODER AND GOODER!

ROBERT HOLLIS

&

LAURIE MONSON

Shackled to Free! Getting Gooder & Gooder

© 2018 Robert Hollis and Laurie Monson.

For information contact; address shackledtofree.com

First Edition: October 2018

Shackled to Free! *Getting Gooder and Gooder*

Cover design by Steve Monson

ISBN-13:
978-1724219336

How is That Working? A Roadmap from Rat Race to Freedom – author Robert Hollis/Max Miller

Are You Stuck? Embracing Change by Releasing Your Potential! - author Laurie Monson

Table of Contents

I dedicate this book to my dear friends all over the world who have shared and trusted me with your struggles, joys, longings, and the desires of your hearts.

WHO IS ROBERT HOLLIS?

I AM PRIVILEGED AND HONORED to co-write this first book in the Shackled to Free series, "Getting Gooder and Gooder!". More than likely, you already know who Robert is, but if not, please let me introduce and share my perspective on who I believe Robert is.

Robert is a highly ambitious and extremely driven leader, and nothing stops him from achieving all he wishes to accomplish in his life. His appetite for growing never ends, and he never goes one day without experiencing something new and then passing it on to others.

He teaches a guidance system for success. He can help you make your dreams come true, avoid dangers, and maximize your opportunities. He teaches how to enrich your life and source and serve everyone to improve theirs. He is real with the public and has unquestionable integrity in his life.

I feel every one of us is unique and Robert Hollis is no exception. He has a belly laugh which makes me smile and laugh every time I hear it. I never grow tired of his infectious laugh and his positive nature. One of his main missions is to bring joy to everyone. He doesn't dwell on the negative news of the world. He stands guard at the door of his mind and consciously chooses the information which goes in it. He doesn't allow anyone to dump anything they want in his mental factory because he knows he has to live with the results. He treats problems as opportunities.

Robert has gone from shackled to free. He internalized all the lessons his mentors taught, became a sponge, and became extremely coachable. If they said, "Jump!" He replied, "How high?" Robert is there to guide you every step of the way. He can and will help you to have steady progress in reaching your own goals and designing the life you choose. Robert is a master at teaching disciplines because he's had to learn them himself. He's not selfish with the ideas which have profoundly changed his life. Matter of fact, he can't wait to share them.

He has created a life he loves and fundamentally influences people with it. You don't have to know Robert personally to be changed and impacted by his message. He is generous sometimes to a fault because he loves to give everything away. He is a significant contributor to others. He has a thirst within him to make a difference. He won't leave you in your mess. He will say "let's do it" and be there for you. Robert's fantastic ability to see the good in lost people is unique.

Robert's message has inalterably changed more lives than anyone can count. He doesn't use a lot of big words which makes him accessible and able to resonate with everyone. It's easy to agree with Robert's words even though you maybe never thought of it in that way. It's a change in your paradigm. When Robert speaks, you can be hit by something simple which will give you a POP (point of passion) because of the way he explains it.

Robert speaks from the heart with his simplistic but powerful messages and has never let his dyslexia keep him from being who God created him to be. He not only is a strategic communicator but strategic in words he sometimes shares even using examples and metaphors out of the Bible. The great thing is you never feel as if Robert is preaching at you. He understands how to drive concepts home. He daily refines his life spiritually as well as personally and follows the teachings of the Bible.

Robert has the innate ability to share and describe the truth, has a positive attitude, and shows optimism in the face of all odds. He knows how to handle the negative and has a no excuse policy for himself and the people he mentors.

Robert exemplifies wisdom and faith deposited in activity and knows and trains that wisdom and faith put to work produces success. He outworks anyone. Robert had the courage thirty years ago to step out of his comfort zone and take the first step. He is not about the next greatest flashy new thing, but proof that documentation beats conversation. He is about mastering the mundane, believing in repetition, working smarter not harder, having forward thinking, and not staying stuck in the past. Robert is willing to plan and work in the spring, so he sees the harvest in the fall.

Robert doesn't learn just for learning sake and realizes self-education makes him a living and a fortune, continually figuring out how to become "gooder and gooder." He knows he needs to invest in himself and always upgrade his skills. He also knows from the greats that continuous learning is the key to unlimited success and growth. He is open to suggestions and open to listening to others who have succeeded in areas he hasn't. Robert has a thirst for ideas which can be life-changing for everyone and wants to create a legacy for his children and grandchildren.

I feel Robert deserves the right to have people listen and follow him because of the value he gives to people on a daily basis. Leadership is influence, and Robert is relationally strong. He is a great listener and listens with a caring heart. He doesn't treat his conversations casually, and if he's talking with you, he is 100% with you not somewhere else in his thoughts, a strength few people have.

Robert's goal is to do more, be more and give more to others than anyone else on earth. Serving others is his secret to abundance. In the Bible, it says if you wish to become great, learn to become the servant of many. Robert believes our greatness comes from serving a large number of people at a deep level. He is such an inspiration to many people including me. Robert is authentic, transparent, and has complete humility as you will see in this book. You will realize Robert cares about you enough that he may get in your face at times but does it in love.

Time is precious to Robert, and he uses it wisely. He has learned how to prioritize and manage his time. Robert has a collection of many experiences, but his favorite is the people who he has made a difference in their lives. His greatest joy is to see his name or hear his name in people's success stories. Every chapter in this book has a Bible verse at the beginning because Robert's faith and love of God is the most important thing to him and he is not ashamed to let everyone know.

Robert's life-long mentor is Jim Rohn. There will never be another Jim Rohn because God broke the mold with him. As far as I'm concerned Robert is his own "Jim Rohn." He follows Jim's philosophies and exemplifies and immolates him, but he is Robert Hollis. I feel God also broke the mold with Robert. We compiled this book from a multitude of Robert's trainings. *Shackled to Free* is a mentorship program on what Robert learned to get "Gooder and Gooder. He will help you see yourself better than you do and transport you into the future of who you can become. He truly walks his walk and is the real thing.

Robert has a unique style and way of getting his message across to people in a way they can understand. As we wrote this book, we didn't want to lose any of this. As you read Robert's book, you will run across many of the "Hollisisms" which make him who he is and draws people to him, such as "getting gooder and gooder."

This book is not only intended to motivate and inspire you but also to help you get "gooder and gooder" as you go from Shackled to Free.

Thanks, Robert for the privilege to share your wisdom with the world! *Laurie Monson*

BLESSED & HIGHLY FAVORED

"Out of my distress I called upon the Lord; the Lord answered me and set me free."

Psalm 118:5

WE LIVE IN THE MOST INCREDIBLE TIME on the planet. I'm excited, blessed, and highly favored to be part of this time. I'm excited to be able to teach you how to build a network and how to give before you get. The world's changing and you need to be a part of the change. You don't want to be left behind!

What are you going to choose? What are you going to get rid of that's not getting you the results you wish? Are you going to do it this year? Are you waiting for January 1st or creating each day as it's the first day of the rest of your life? It's easy to do, but also easy not to do. It's your choice.

If you are sick, tired, and disgusted, you are going to do something about it. If you don't, you are not at the right time in your life. That's ok. That's why I love you, and I will continue to keep giving value, continue praying for you and hoping it becomes the right time for you in your life. Timing is everything. We always hear about these serendipity times where you get it and wham!

Regardless of your spiritual beliefs, every religious belief says all things are possible! It doesn't mean a few things, or most things are possible. It says all things are possible for those who believe. What if you placed confidence in a proven online system and the person running the system? When you have faith it is possible, and others have done the system with success, you will say, "If they can do it, I can do it." They have no doubt in their abilities to do it, and that's where the magic happens. This is how the magic happened for me, and how I received a POP (point of passion).

When I understood the principles of *Science of Getting Rich* by Wallace Wattles and understood the principles of Think and *Grow Rich*, I realized how blessed and highly favored and unstoppable I was. Do you believe you are invincible and blessed?

I can help anyone get want they want in life, but I have a hard time finding people who know what they want. My question to you is, do you know what you want? Why are you not doing the things you know to do? Are your limiting beliefs holding you back? Everything you do has to do with a level of faith. If you don't believe in what you are doing, you aren't going to act on it.

Is there someone in your life who has declared you wouldn't amount to anything? Do you continuously dwell on all the negative things that person has spoken about you over the years? We all think we can get rid of negativity, but the only way is to reprogram our thinking.

You are out of the ordinary and unique. You have the ability, just as I, to inspire other people to be great. You can encourage other people to dream again. How many people do you know who need your inspiration?

People make decisions based on emotions, and how they feel about other people. We come from an environment and culture where we don't make resolutions because it feels good; because we can't trust that feeling. We say we don't have enough information. Does this sound like you?

You are a winner! I'm proud of you and give you permission to be happy, successful, wealthy, give to charity, and travel the world. Anything you want to do, I give you my stamp of approval now to do it. If no one has ever given you permission to do great things in your life, be a winner, and go from shackled to free, I just did. My mentor did this for me, and I'm returning the favor.

The key to success is simple. You must fall in love with your vision and dream. You must find people who have succeeded in what you want to do, become disciplined, and coachable. You must believe in your heart if God has allowed other people to pull it off, He's not keeping it from you. The only thing that is stopping you is you. It's right now in your grasp. You must follow the proven system laid out for you. My book is about Getting Gooder and Gooder and going from shackled to free. Enjoy!

Robert Hollis

SHACKLED TO FREE!

GETTING GOODER & GOODER!

PREFACE:

As I stopped the car, I heard a little voice in the back seat, "Daddy, why aren't you driving our car into the parking lot of our apartment building?" Such shame blanketed me as I lied to my son because I couldn't tell him that I was hiding our car from the repo man. As I sat with my head on the steering wheel in tears, so many memories flooded my mind.

The judge struck his gavel, "Robert Hollis I sentence you to five years in the Federal Penitentiary, two to serve and three suspended. Take him away!"

Sitting alone in my prison cell, I asked myself, "How could these past seventeen years have gotten me to this point? I have one of two choices. I can take the time and learn from my past, or I can get bitter and come out in two years the same or in worse shape than I am now." As I sat with tears rolling down my face, seventeen years of voices haunted my mind.

"You have one hour to mow the lawn! If you don't get it mowed, I will beat you!" Knowing I couldn't accomplish this gargantuan task, I braced for yet another beating.

Loud piercing sirens came closer as flashing red lights pulled up to my house. "We need to take your mom to the hospital; your dad beat her horribly." As the ambulance pulled away, the police handcuffed my dad and took him away. My brothers and I were left alone.

The police showed up at our house. "We are taking your mom to jail because she didn't protect you and your brothers."

The social worker took me aside and said, "Robert, you must go to foster care because your mom and dad are in jail. You and your brothers will be in separate foster homes. Say goodbye to them."

Sitting in my prison cell with my head in my hands, I had to decide if I would let my crappy story of physical, emotional, and sexual abuse define the rest of my life. I prayed, "God, please transform my life."

"Robert, you are "special." You have dyslexia." All I heard was, "Robert, you are worthless and won't amount to anything."

The thoughts continued to flood my mind, as I replayed the van slipping off the hoist and attempting to keep it from falling. The doctor's voice haunts me, "You must find a different career because you can't be on your legs anymore. Your mechanic career is over."

"If you don't pay your rent by the end of the month, you and your son are out. You are a couple of months behind in payments, and at the end of the month, we will be moving your belongings out. The sheriff will be there to escort you out."

"Son, you must go live with your mom. I can't take care of you anymore." Is my life even worth living?

I wish I knew, as I sat in my car reliving my past, that these horrible, scattered memories would not haunt me for the rest of my life. I could never have imagined how blessed and highly favored my life would turn out to be, and how many people I would have the opportunity to help. Have you let your bad memories and failures define your future? Let me walk you through the concepts I learned on my journey from Shackled to Free

-CHAPTER ONE-

RESET YOUR LIFE

"This is the day that the Lord has made; let us rejoice and be glad in it."

Psalm 118:24

Most people can change their mental state and their emotions. If you are in the wrong mental state and wrong psychological attitude when you work on building your dreams, do you believe that it is as effective as it could be if you were in a more positive state of mind? Do you know of certain individuals that as soon as they walk in the room, it's like the lights dim? I don't know what is going on in your mind right now, but regardless of that, I'm going to show you how you can change your attitude. Do you hang around dream stealers? It's not only the ability to change your state and your emotions, but it also depends on the people you have around you.

On December 31st are you excited a New Year is coming? Do you celebrate the previous year and anticipate the coming year? Are you excited to say, "Off with the old, on with the new?" What is unique about a new year is it allows you to forget about yesterday. Everyone permits you to start new. You get to change, and even the world thinks positively about New Year's resolutions. New Year's non-resolutions are a new type of resolutions. What are you not willing to give up for the New Year? Examples could be happiness, success, health... January 1st is a new day and new chapter in your life. You have this ability, as I do, to accomplish this every month by not waiting until January 1st. Most entrepreneurs say, "It's a new month, and I get to start over." Why can't you change that to a week? Why couldn't you change that to every day? What if you could take the excitement, toss the cares away, and knock the dust off your shoes every day?

For those of you who are spiritual, the Scripture says, "Take all your cares and cast them on me." I walk around my house telling my family, "Today is the first day of the rest of our lives."

PUSH YOUR RESET BUTTON

You can create the excitement you feel on December 31st as you anticipate the New Year. You can regenerate that every day. Hit the reset button, shut your thoughts off, reboot, and start again. You can have the right attitude, get rid of all the old mindsets, and figure out your new resolutions.

Reprogramming and rebooting your brain are processes. Let's say I gave you a brand-new laptop computer, you started it, and nothing happened. Before I gave you the laptop, I pointed out, "You need to listen to my words; everything I'm going to have you complete is simple. This computer runs well, but you need to delete all the past programming. The computer needs rebooting, and you must install the latest programs. Once you do this, your computer will be like new." Your life is the same. Listen to my words, "Everything I am going to have you complete is simple. You must continually work on your mind and regularly reboot and start over."

The way you gain confidence, get rid of feeling unworthy, believe, and have faith if other people can achieve success, you can too, is you must go through the same process. No one can shortcut the process by using a magic wand. That's not the way it works.

It takes a paradigm shift, a reframing in your mind, where it now becomes yours and becomes a fact. When you know a point to be true, believe it with all your heart and soul, you will have confidence. Your self-esteem, belief, and your ability to become successful will grow. Your knowledge of how to do it is usually not the way. If you knew already what you needed to know to get where you wanted to go, then why aren't you there?

You can reboot your life every day. Turn on the new programming, and it will be effectively virus-free. It's running the recent programs without overheating, locking up, or shutting down. You must reframe things in your life by recording yourself and listening to the defeating and self-sabotaging stuff you are saying about yourself.

What if every night you excitedly wrote in your journal about your gratefulness? Daily you reframed your mind on a positive level. It wasn't a perfect day, but you can say, "I could have accomplished more, but I'm going to be happy with what I accomplished." You give yourself a pep talk and say, "I'm going to get a little bit better every day in every way." As I like to say, "I'm getting gooder and gooder."

Congratulate yourself on achieving what you have accomplished. We don't pat ourselves on the back enough. We always feel we are losers, not producing enough, constantly guilty because we didn't achieve this and didn't do that. We say, "I should have been there already. I should have contacted more people. I should of...." You must stop mistreating yourself! Stop "shoulding" yourself to death!

Every day in your journal keep track of what makes you grateful. You need to give yourself credit today for what you accomplished, and tomorrow will be the first day of the rest of your life.

YOU ARE DESIGNED TO CHOOSE

What are you going to choose? What are you going to get rid of that's not getting you the results you wish? Are you going to get rid of them this year? Are you waiting for January 1st or creating each day as it's the first day of the rest of your life? You can have the experience you wish. It's easy to do but also easy not to do. It's your choice.

Are you mentally ok with resetting once a year because everyone else always does? You will be able to find out if you are a leader or a follower by how you answered that question. Can you imagine if you woke every day and asked, "What are my resolutions for today?" If you don't, you get to wake the next day, and it's Groundhog Day unless you can change it by getting a little better every day. It's called kaizen, which is the consistent effort and never-ending improvement to get "gooder and gooder" every day.

STOP IT!

Your year starts right now. Have you ever decided you needed to set New Year's goals for your business/life and all your goals would begin on January 1st? It doesn't happen at the beginning of January because you can't reach out to people at this time because of New Year's Eve parties. You set a goal for February. February is getting too close to Valentine's Day. People don't want to talk to you then, because they are planning on Valentine surprises for spouses or significant others. You expect to start your goals after Valentine's Day.

Before you know it, Easter comes, and that is set aside for church and family and Easter egg extravaganzas for the kids. After Easter, it's time for taxes. People stress out at tax time, so you can't talk to them then. Then school is about out, and summer vacation is coming. You know summer vacation nobody is home, and everybody is busy traveling. You have decided to take off for the summer because winter ended up being long and hard; you deserve some relaxation. Then oh my, it's fall. Too much happens in the fall with school getting ready to start, and nobody will want to talk to you when school is starting. Now it's Thanksgiving, and it's hard to get people to focus on anything during the holidays because they want to relax and take a little bit of time off. Then it's Black Friday and Cyber Monday. You have some shopping to get in order. Before you even know it, Christmas is here. We can't do anything during Christmas. New Years is coming up... Stop it!

My challenge to you is to celebrate the first day of the rest of your life every day. I have been achieving this for many years, so January 1st is no big deal for me. The world expects people to set resolutions on January 1st every year. Always remember if other people are doing it, you can do it too. You need to find documented people, like me, who have taken the time to help other people be successful. If you haven't picked a mentor yet, it's the first day of the rest of your life. Check out: www.documentationbeatsconversation.com. You will learn a method that will keep you motivated, inspired, and jacked out of your mind. It will give you energy and passion.

Helping people go from existing to living a life that they always dreamed of isn't work for me. There isn't anything better in the world. I don't know what game you are playing, but my game is helping people who want the best out of their lives develop an incredible lifestyle. I know you can have that and more. Remember, today is the first day of the rest of your life.

God loves you, I love you, and I pray for your success daily!

<u>Questions for Reflection:</u>

*Where in your life, as you work on building your dreams, are you in the wrong mental state? What can you change to be in a better state of mind?

*What are you grateful for and how can you reframe your mind on a positive level?

*Where in your life are you "shoulding" yourself?

*What are you going to get rid of because it's not giving you the results you wish?

CHAPTER TWO

DO YOU BELIEVE?

"Now faith is confidence in what we hope for and assurance about what we do not see."

Hebrews 11:1

Many people struggle in life. Are you one of them? The reason you may be struggling is your lack of belief. Not only do you need to believe you can do this; you must understand what you are doing can be done. If you don't think you can do it and it's possible, nothing else matters. Belief is the core of everything. If you don't keep the faith, you won't go into action. When you don't have hope, you second-guess yourself and limiting beliefs set in. When you believe the work is simple, you get rid of fear.

Many people believe they need to get an education which teaches them exactly what to do. It's not what to do; it's the belief you can do it. If you genuinely believe you can do something, you will do it. You don't think about whether you will be good at it. You know it will take practice. You know if other people can do it, you can do it. It's all about believing YOU can also do it.

Think back to when you decided to drive. First, you saw someone driving. You thought if other people can do it, I can do it. You took the pursuit not only to get the knowledge, but you found the right instructor, completed all the practice you needed, and finally after much practice you learned to drive. When you become an entrepreneur, you need to do similar things as you completed when you learned to drive. You may have worked your whole life as a coin-operated person, and now you decide to become an entrepreneur. First, understand if other people are successful at becoming an entrepreneur and doing it, YOU can do it.

A significant number of people, regardless if they are involved in online sales, network marketing, or whatever company or industry they are with, are doing the same thing you are trying to do. If they can do it, you can do it. It doesn't make a difference what company you joined. It doesn't matter your race or language you speak, nor if you are male, female, where you live, or your spiritual beliefs. People have been successful with what you want to do.

FISHING STARTS WITH BELIEF AND A DECISION

People tell success stories to get you to realize you can do it. You will hear "look at this single mom who changed her life. Look at this guy from your country that had success." They continuously share stories with you, and it gets you excited because you realize if they can do it; you can also do it.

Have you heard the parable about teaching other people to fish? The whole concept is, do you believe you can catch fish? Other people have success fishing, why

14

aren't you? You buy a rod, tackle, go to the lake, and cast your line out.

You say, "I'm not getting any bites."

Finally, after several days, you humble yourself, talk to a professional angler, and he tells you, "The fish aren't biting where you are fishing."

You say, "Ok, where are the fish?"

The expert angler tells you, "They are over there," as he points to a different area.

You begin fishing and say, "I'm not catching anything. Fishing doesn't work for me." You are close to giving up.

The expert fisherman tells you, "You aren't going to catch fish with the bait you are using."

You get frustrated and give up and say, "I can't catch fish! How many rules are there? Fishing doesn't work for people like me."

Fishing and attracting people start with your belief and decision to do it. Once you decide you can do it, you must work on you and your confidence that you can do this. If you don't believe you can be successful, how will you reach your goals? You must also follow the system of those before you who have had success because following a proven system is vital.

YES, YOU CAN!

Remember thoughts and words are things. You must change your thoughts to switch your words. As you say your words, your ears hear them, they resonate with your spirit, heart, and soul, and then change occurs.

The first goal is to figure out your desires. If you look through your entire life, you can see stories repeatedly where you wanted something badly enough, believed you could do it, went out, and did it. Yes, I think you can do it again!

People look at other people who are successful, and the one thing every one of these people has in common is at one time they weren't successful. They weren't the same person they are today. Millionaires at one time started with no money. Look at things you can do. Start getting little victories and go from win to win. There's not a doubt in my mind that you can have success. Instead of waiting every day for the days, weeks, and months to go past, you must start by saying, "Yes, I can have success! Yes, I can be an author! Yes, I can replace my income! Yes, I can be a marketer! Yes, I can be happy! Yes, I can travel! Yes, I can build my relationships! Yes, I can learn to love myself!"

TOO MANY FACTS!

When you as an entrepreneur think about the best thing to remember when researching anything, what is your first thought? Most people feel the most important thing to know is the facts. It's incredible to me when people ask me how they can be successful; they want to know about things I feel don't matter, the facts. "What is the price of the product? How does the payment plan work? Does the company have a sizzle product? All these things are secondary or even third, fourth, and fifth in the line of importance. If you are struggling, I feel you are missing the concept "thoughts are things". Don't get hung up on the facts and miss the big picture in life.

The reason you talk about the facts in your company, for example, the product, pay plan and company information, is because you haven't yet fully believed in yourself. You are still trying to convince yourself you can have success. If you believed you could do it; you wouldn't be talking about facts. If you only talk about the data, you are messing up big time. You need to talk about the results the product can give to the person or the service you can give. You need to talk about the lifestyle they can have, and the freedom they can have by being an entrepreneur. Give them the picture of how different their lives could be if they could do anything, anytime, with anyone they wanted. You haven't opened them up to the possibilities of traveling the world and giving to their families. You haven't shared with them how much they will be able to give to charities if they wish.

As soon as you start talking about the facts, people's eyes glass over, and they quit listening. When you give the data to people, they always ask another question. See if other people are doing it, you can do it! The reason you aren't getting the results when talking to other people is that you talk about what it is. You aren't saying what it will do for them. You haven't shared what it has done for you. You say, "It hasn't done anything for me." The reason it hasn't done anything for you is that you haven't believed. You need to ask yourself, "If I don't believe, what do I need to do every day to build my belief and faith?"

When you believe what you are doing, talking to people is easy!

DECISIONS BASED ON EMOTIONS

Why is it we always need to know the facts; even though we know the facts don't matter? People make decisions based on emotions. People make judgments based on the way they feel about people. We come from an environment and culture where we don't make decisions because it feels good. We think we can't trust that feeling. We always think we don't have enough information. Is this you?

People say to me, "Hey Robert, do you know about the compensation plan?"

I tell them, "No, I don't."

Puzzled, they ask me, "What do you mean?"

I tell them, "I understand compensation plans change all the time. My goal is to get to the first level of my company and teach others to get to that level. Usually, when I help others get to the first level; it will push me to the next level. It's amazing how compensation plans work! If I help those people and their people get to my level, I get to go to the next level. It's all based on volume and based on me talking to people, asking if they would be interested in any way, shape, or form of doing something which will make them happier, feel better, and have extra money. It's that simple!"

What if you know all the answers? If your goal is to know all the facts, when do you know all the facts? The answer is never! If you shoot for an objective, you should at least pick an achievable one.

Have you been in a relationship? Did you get all the facts before starting it? No! Have you had children? Did you get all the information before becoming a parent? No! How about getting involved in your first job, did you get all the data? The answer is again, No! Everything we've been successful with, we never figured out all the facts about it. Isn't it right if you didn't get all the facts about everything else in your life, you are using this now as an excuse not to go into action? Do you say, "If I knew all the facts?" Guess what? You are never going to know all the facts!

PICK A NEW MENTOR

The reason I earned $10,000 my first 45 days and made $258,000 my first year is I found a mentor. He convinced me I could be an entrepreneur by sharing stories of other people he taught who also had success. He talked about what his mentorship and training could do for me. He instilled a sense of belief in me where I became unstoppable.

Did the mentor you followed in the past year help you get the results you deserved? If not, pick a new mentor. Many people teach things which aren't duplicable. They are not good at marketing or today's psychology. You should try something different. The definition of insanity is to keep doing the same thing over and over and expecting a different result.

Two groups of people will be reading this. The first group always finds a way to think it's not going to work for them. They say, "This can't work!" They don't believe it and are skeptical. These people don't realize the people they grew up with and hang around with now, make a difference. These people don't believe anything. Guess what? Thoughts are things.

The second group of people is similar to me. They believe everything. Trust me, I understand, much we hear or read is not true, but I like being on the other side. I love being optimistic and believing things are true. If I find out they are not, it's no big deal. I can shake it off quickly; it's fantastic! Which group best exemplifies you?

Do you believe in you? You must start feeling you can be successful, and make more money then you've ever dreamed possible by helping people become more aware. You need to help people become optimists and believe in the possibilities that they can fulfill the dreams God has for them. You must show them they can give to the charities of their choice if they wish.

We live in what I believe the most incredible time on the planet. I'm excited and blessed to be part of this time. I'm excited to be able to teach you how to have success and how to give before you get. The world's changing and you need to be a part of the change, so don't stay behind!

God loves you, I love you, and pray for your success daily!

Questions for Reflection:

*Do you believe you can reach the goals you have set for yourself?

*Are you using the excuse that you don't have enough facts keep you from going into action?

*What do you need to do every day to build your belief and faith?

*Are you more an optimist or pessimist?

-CHAPTER THREE-

YOU ARE SPECIAL!

"Yet you, Lord are our Father. We are the clay; you are the potter; we are all the work of your hand."

Isaiah 64:8

Has someone ever told you, "You are special? When I grew up and attended high school, I had to wear the label "special." because the experts didn't know how to diagnose my dyslexia. I would look at a picture of a "th" sound, and I knew the sound and could say it. They would show a picture of a thumb, and I would say thumb. They would show the word "thumb", and I would say "tum". I couldn't see the "h". I attended speech therapy with the "special kids" because at that time they couldn't diagnose my disability. I knew I was special all along and still realize I am unique. Today I'm thankful God created me to be unique and wouldn't want to be anyone else. You need to find the special part about yourself. God created one of you, so you should act unique. You need to want to be you and no one else.

I realized early on reading and spelling weren't going to be my forte. I knew English was not going to be my strength. I immediately signed up for the classes people mentioned I excelled in, like math and science. My talent was working with my hands. At fifteen years of age, I began working as a mechanic building and repairing mini bikes. I bought mini-bikes, motorcycles, and snowmobiles with my paper route money, and fixed and sold them. I built a car someone gave me for free and had it running before I received my driver's license.

The reason I share this is that I leaned toward something I was naturally good at which fit my personality and strengths. Are you always trying to do things which don't match who you are? Henry Ford couldn't read or write, and he pointed out, "If you think you can't, you can't and if you think you can, you can." Do you say, "I don't like doing it that way, or I'm not good at that?" You need to say I can instead of I can't. What is your mindset?

TIMING IS EVERYTHING

I went to a trade school where I received my degree in auto mechanics and auto mechanic engineering. Since I was good at mechanics, I dreamed of someday working on race cars and being a crew chief. My mind focused on this dream, so I didn't focus on any other career. Timing is everything! Nothing was going to get in my way or at least that's what I thought.

No person who will ever read this book, not even my mentor, could have derailed me from my vision and my dreams. My goal was to be an excellent auto mechanic and automotive engineer. My ultimate goal was to be a crew

24

chief. Because of the timing, no one had the skills to change my mind. If anyone had tried to recruit me during that time, no line I know of could have worked on me. You must understand if a person is already excited, focused on their dream, motivated, confident, and doing things on their craft every day; you can't say anything to change their mind.

When you talk to people, do you run into people who just got a job? Are you running into people who are focused on getting a degree or people who love the job they have? Contrary to what you might believe, some people like their career or job. People, who are already involved in an entrepreneurial endeavor and love it, may not have any thought of changing to another company. I know people called into the ministry, and you aren't going to get them unfocused no matter what you say. What we try to do is change their mind. That's dumb!

NOW, WHAT AM I GOING TO DO?

Again, why is timing in my story important? Suddenly, a van falls on me, and I go on Workman's Comp. No big deal. I had to get surgery on my knee and go through rehab. Workman's Comp and rehab almost took away my services three times because I wouldn't stop exercising my leg. I put flour bags and sugar bags on my ankle, and I lifted them at the same time I had a cast on my leg. They continued to lecture me, "When you are in a cast, your muscles and your leg starts shrinking. You must quit over exercising." In my mind, to get back to my vision and dreams, I needed to be serious about working out and rehabilitation. I thought nothing could stop me. Do you struggle and not do what you need to do? Let me ask you, "What the heck do you want, and do you want it bad enough where nothing can stop you?"

Let's go back to my story and timing being everything. The doctor does an MRI to check on my leg. Unfortunately, the surgery had failed; and I needed to have another one. At this time, I had experienced seven months on Workman's Comp which would be ending shortly. The doctors told me I needed to retrain and find a different career which didn't require I stand all day because they reminded me I wasn't going to be able to support weight on my leg. People with degrees and medical doctors with white coats must know more than me, right? They told me I couldn't be a mechanic anymore and my goal as a crew chief might not exist anymore. Wow! I felt my life was over.

Now, listen! Here is the time in my life where I became humbled, and my mind opened like a parachute. Up to this point, I still had a hope of being a mechanic and crew chief. For the first time in my life, I needed to think about something else I was qualified to do. When I say timing is everything, I asked myself how I could learn something new which wasn't going to take physical ability. My timing was becoming right.

HAVING AN OPEN MIND

No thoughts entered my mind about becoming an entrepreneur, doing marketing, or building an organization. No ideas came into my mind about doing personal development to better myself, but I opened my mind just a little. I became humble, and I'm bold enough to tell you I spent much time reconnecting with my Creator on my one healthy knee. I prayed hard every day and listened openly for an answer.

If you were watching the movie of my life, suddenly Sean Hennigan called me and connected me with his mentor. Now, the timing became correct! What's the point of my story? I had already humbled myself and was desperate when I met my mentor, Bill Gouldd. I did what Bill instructed me to do. He told me, "Go out, talk to people, and ask them to do you a huge personal favor. Ask them if they know anyone who is interested in making some additional income. Tell them you are working directly with me, and I am expanding a company. Get them in front of me doing an effective presentation."

I said, "Yes, Sir!"

"Robert, you have to follow this treasure map. Don't go sideways. Don't try to change anything. Don't reinvent the wheel. Just do this with me for 90 days, and I promise you your whole life will change." "Can you do that for me?"

Without hesitating, I said, "I can."

"The first thing that you have to do is you have to get excited."

"I am excited!"

"You have to stay excited."

Staying excited is hard. People's words are one thing, but their enthusiasm, their excitement behind their passion, all of that is more than the words. Wouldn't you agree? So, you could say the same words, but if the words aren't spoken with the belief that you can make it happen for yourself, it won't happen. You must get ex it simple, pay attention, and don't add anything to it, because confused people do nothing.

The most important thing for you to master is discipline; work on this first. I worked harder than I worked for anybody else because I realized I now worked for myself. I believed my mentor and his ability to help other people because he had testimonials. My timing became perfect!

I have people all the time say to me, "You wouldn't believe how many people I talked to, and they weren't interested. They joined my team and hadn't brought in one person. They won't plug into the training. I have people who won't follow the system."

I reply, "Their timing, isn't right!"

IS YOUR TIMING NOW?

You can't say the wrong thing to the right person. Others will tell you this statement isn't true. I believe, because of my personal story, that it's true.

Sean asked me, "Have you heard of Amway?"

"No, I haven't."

"Well, it's not Amway and its legal!"

This script wasn't what the company taught, but it worked on me because the timing was right. If you are excited, know how to promote, and edify, people will run you over to get to the person who has the results and success. You will know you are talking to the right people at the right time when you ask them to follow a system; they do it immediately and get in front of your mentor. Bottom line timing is everything!

You must sort quickly. At a time in my life no matter what you said to me, you wouldn't have gotten my attention. Also, a time came in my life where you couldn't say anything wrong to Robert Hollis because I wanted to change. Now, let's talk about you. Do you believe the timing is right in your life? Do you feel you are a leader? Are you coachable and have vision and goals? Do you have an excellent work ethic? Are you a winner?

BE TEACHABLE

Are you willing to follow instructions and say as little as possible to as many people as you can but are doing the exact opposite? If you are doing the opposite, your time is not now! Just because you got involved in an entrepreneurial business opportunity, loved the concept of marketing, liked the idea of building your brand, loved the product and company, doesn't mean this is the right time for you. Wow! Does this surprise you that I am saying this?

When my mentor said, "You want to work with me, read *Think and Grow Rich* by Napoleon Hill." I immediately bought the book, read it, and applied it with no excuses. I've mentioned I don't like reading and I did it anyway. Why? My mentor told me to do it, and I knew if I wanted to work with my mentor, I needed to do everything he said. I wanted to work with my mentor more than I didn't want to read the book. I wanted to work with a guy who made $62,000 a month and helped others make six figures. I knew by working with him; I could have success as others had.

Early on, I realized leaders are readers, and I found another book which changed my life, *Science of Getting Rich*. I tell people who reach out to me I will send them free audios and the free e-book for *Think and Grow Rich* and *Science of Getting Rich*. All they must do is contact me and ask me to send it to them. Few people I offer this gift to follow my instructions. Few people want it bad enough as I did.

I give anyone who asks value for free, but only a small group of people genuinely want to better themselves. Why do most people I mentor refuse to do something that's easy to do and life-changing? The reason is they get distracted, and something else always comes up. They might have good intentions to better their lives, but suddenly all these things come to their minds, and they are not at the right place at the right time. Also, it's easier not to do.

I have this large group of people who won't ask for this link. Another group of people will ask for the link, and when I send it to them, everything is more critical and distracting to them than changing their thoughts. I'm still working with people, on a personal basis, who say, "I can't get rid of my stinking thinking! I'm stuck! I'm struggling! I can't stay in the groove! I can't... I can't... I can't..." Are you kidding me?

My mentor told me, "Listen, Robert, you have a problem with your self- esteem."

"What are you talking about?"

"You constantly worry about what other people think and say about you. You have low confidence issues which you need to take care of."

I didn't tell him he was wrong or didn't know what he was saying. I didn't ignore what he pointed out to me. I asked him, "How can I change my insecurities?"

He responded, "That's exactly the right question!" My mentor made statements to see my reaction to criticism. He did this to see if I would accept correction.

MORE VALUABLE THAN MONEY

Mentors know time is more valuable than money. Mentors request you to do something which seems insignificant and straightforward to see if you are coachable, ready to learn, and can follow instructions. Mentors guide people who don't like where they are in life.

When I asked my mentor what I could do about my self-esteem issue, he answered, "You need to go to the library and get a book by Og Mandino called *The Greatest Miracle in the World*."

I told him, "I will get it immediately." I was so desperate at that point and time in my life that I was willing to do what my mentor showed me. My mentor didn't give me a bunch of assignments. He gave me small ones to see if I would do "wax on, wax off," from the Karate Kid. I connected with my mentor and told him I read it.

He asked me, "What did you think about *The God Memorandum*?"

"I cried, like a baby, for hours. Just as the book mentioned; I'm reading it every day."

He reminded me, "Robert, you need to read it until you have confidence, self-esteem, until you feel you are the greatest miracle in the world, until you fall in love with yourself, until you don't care about other people's thoughts, and until you don't care about other people's words. That's how many times you should be reading it."

Are you a person who doubts who you are? If this is you, you better be listening to or reading *The Greatest Miracle in the World*. Should you listen to it or read it more than once? I don't know. How bad is your life? How disgusted are you with your life right now? Do you have the same crap different day? How sick and tired are you?

NOT DISGUSTED ENOUGH

If you are sick, tired, and disgusted with your life, you need to do something about it. If you don't, you are not at the right time in your life. That's ok. That's why I love you, keep giving you value, continue praying for you, and hope it becomes the right time for you in your life. Timing is everything. We always hear about these serendipity times where you get it and then wham!

The point in my life which made me the person I am today is when I didn't want to lie to my son and make excuses why I hid the car from the repo man. When you listen to every successful person, they had a day when they became disgusted with their life and declared, "No More!" That's when it was their time.

If you are not doing something you are supposed to be doing every day to make your life better in every way; it's not your time. Don't beat yourself up! You are just not disgusted enough!

God loves you, I love you, and pray for your success daily!

Questions for Reflection:

*Where in your life do you feel you are "special"?

*When in your life have you become humbled and your mind opened up like a parachute?

*How do you react to constructive criticism?

*Are you at a point in your life where you say, "enough is enough"?

-CHAPTER FOUR-

WHO DO YOU ATTRACT?

"If it is to encourage, then give encouragement; if it is giving, then give generously; if it is to lead, do it diligently; if it's to show mercy, do it cheerfully."

Romans 12:8

We encounter four distinct types of people. The first group is "know-it-alls". They are the right-fighters. They feel they know everything. I love Jim Rohn's quote about these people, "Success leaves clues." These people say "I read that book. I watched that video. I've been through the Secret many times. I know what to say to people. I've joined many companies. I know all this." Their life sucks, they have no real friends, no one follows them, they aren't making any money, and they live a lie. They would rather fight for the right to be right, rather than fight for happiness, wealth, love, contribution, and friendships.

Do you feel you are a know-it-all and a right fighter? Do you think you are a leader? A definition of a leader is when you look behind you and people are following you. The next step is those who follow you convert into leaders.

I used to be a right fighter. I was the type of guy if I found out in our debate or argument I was wrong, I wouldn't admit to being wrong but would say, "I misunderstood what you said."

Do you spend your time with know-it-alls and right-fighters? Why do you do this?

BEING AN "ASK-HOLE"

Another group of people is the people who ask non-stop questions. Why do we always ask questions? We ask questions because people think we should. It makes us sound intelligent.

An example for the ladies is you go out in search for the perfect dress and shoes. You spot the ideal outfit in the store window. It's the bomb! You try on this beautiful dress, and it makes you feel as if you are twenty pounds lighter and it fits perfect. You know this dress and pair of shoes is coming home with you. Do you pay for them immediately? No, you feel it's crazy if you become emotional about something, get excited, or want to buy it right away. You ask questions which don't matter. You ask the clerk, "How much is it? What kind of fabric is it made of? Can this be dry cleaned? What is your return policy? Is this going to go on sale soon?"

These are all questions we ask only to ask. They mean nothing, but we do it because everybody else is asking questions which make you think you also need to. We go from trying to be independent to a "sheeple." You go out to buy a car. You find the perfect car which you have been searching for for months. It has every feature you want and is the right price, but you begin asking questions,

"What's the fuel mileage? What's the resale value? What's the warranty? Does it come with other features?" Come On! We do this because we feel as if we should, and we don't want to look stupid. None of that matters!

Some people ask questions for no reason at all, and some people ask questions because they are interested and want to know the details because they are a seeker. You have people who ask questions with no intention whatsoever of doing anything. I call these people "ask-holes." They say, "Robert, what do you do? How do you do this?" These people already know the answers but refuse to do anything except ask questions. How do you get people out of asking questions which don't matter? You don't answer their questions. You need to learn to answer questions with questions.

If someone says to me, "Robert, what about the pay plan?"

I ask them, "Is this the most important thing to you? The pay plan may be important for you to decide, but it wasn't important to me. I can send you over a video from the leaders of the company who will walk you through the payment plan. Also, you can go to the company website and print out the pdf."

The person asking the question wants to know where they can get the answer. I tell the person, "Great question! The Customer Service Department of this company is amazing, and they would be happy to answer your questions."

Do I know the answers to these questions? Yes, most the time I do, but I want people to learn to plug in where they can get the resources. When people ask me questions about the pay plan, I tell them I'm not an expert. When people ask me questions about the company, I let them know I'm not an expert and don't own the company. You need to get good at knowing where you can go for answers and where you can point, guide, and direct other people to the resources and the solutions. In our minds, we think we look stupid or incompetent if we don't know the answers or we know the answers and don't answer their questions. Don't make yourself the deal! Use the system already in place and the experts.

IT DOESN'T HURT BAD ENOUGH

You also have the group of people who are comfortable. These are the people who are in the wrong place at the wrong time. I attract countless people. Some of them are "know-it-alls," right fighters, "ask-holes," and some are too comfortable. If you are comfortable, you aren't disgusted with your life. You tell people you are disgusted, but, it's not bad enough to change.

This person reminds me of the guy who walks up to the farmer sitting on the porch with his dog. The dog is crying and crying. The guy asks the farmer, "What is wrong with your dog?"

The farmer says, "My dog is lying on a nail."

The guy asks the farmer, "Why doesn't your dog get up and move?"

The farmer tells the guy, "It doesn't hurt bad enough!"

The comfortable people don't have it bad enough to do the things they need to do to improve their lives. I run into these people all the time. All they want to do is show me they are active by going through the actions of some training or going to seminar after seminar. They've been with many companies without results. Their timing isn't right because they are too comfortable.

I'm not saying they don't want things to work out, but that's not enough. Let me tell you a secret. I want to lose weight. I buy the Bow Flex, elliptical, weights, sauna, and all the equipment I need to get in shape and lose weight, but the bottom line is the timing isn't right; I'm too comfortable.

CHANGE BEGINS FROM THE INSIDE OUT

Another group of people, you will run across, is the people pleasers. Being happy, wealthy, loving, and being a go-giver is an inside job. People pleasers struggle with what they believe others think about them. They struggle with what people say or the questions people ask. They worry about what they need to tell other people. One of the saddest things I've ever seen, so if you are a people pleaser, I can help you deal with it.

Most super successful people experienced something tragic in their lives and dealt with bullying. The difference between successful people and others is successful people don't listen or care about what others say or think about them. These thoughts of them don't deserve a millisecond of their time. It's ok to listen to what other people say if it's kind, encouraging, and lifting you up. Be sure to surround yourself with those people all the time but don't listen to the negativity.

IT'S NONE OF YOUR BUSINESS

In Chapter 3, I shared about my label "special" in school and attending an auto mechanic class. How did I graduate with my disability? I was resourceful. I found people and made deals with them. I told them I would help them with their mechanical stuff if they would take my English and required subjects for me. My teachers wanted me to learn the art of communication. I felt I already knew how to communicate. "Can you hear me? Well, I can hear you; communications completed."

Every time I hung around kids, they gossiped about me. "Hey, that's one of those foster kids. He doesn't have a dad, and he's special." I had to learn at an early age what people said about me and gossiped behind my back to others about me, wasn't any of my business.

What people say about you is none of your business either. If you don't feel right in your skin, you won't feel you are the greatest miracle in the world. You haven't fallen in love with yourself and learned not to care what other people think of you. You are in trouble, and it will hold you back because you will become paralyzed by worrying about what other people think and say about you.

ARE YOU A SECRET AGENT?

If I talked to your family, your friends, and the people who are closest to you, would they know your career or business? Are you worried about what they think? If you are a secret agent, good chance you aren't fulfilling your dreams. Do you live the life you are supposed to live? Do you give to charity? Do you give to the people you love and make sure you spend time with them? Are you traveling the world and living to the fullest and experiencing your best life?

You worry about what people say and think about you and most the time they are not saying anything. People do not sit around thinking about what you are doing and asking others what you are doing. They don't have the time. They are too busy wrapped up in their craziness trying to figure out their own lives. When you first came into this world, got married, had children, or became an entrepreneur, you didn't get an owner's manual, and they didn't either. Really, the opinions or labels we give ourselves are the only ones that honestly matter.

I want you to think of a place called "your happy place." Think about times when you are happy, and everything is going well. You must think about the fact there are Darth Vader's in the world. Their number one goal is to pull you out of your game, presence, joy, and pull you out of your box. When you fall into it and allow them to take a millisecond from you, they won; you lost.

NOT EVERYONE LOVES ME, AND THAT'S OK

Do you believe everyone loves Robert Hollis and no one says anything negative about me? Wouldn't that be awesome? A world where everyone likes me and likes everything I do. Wow! Do you realize if people aren't writing or saying something about you good or bad, you aren't doing anything? Are you listening to me? You don't want to worry about the dreadful things people might be saying about you, but you also don't want to get prideful about the good things they are saying.

I have people all the time come to me and say, "Have you heard what so and so said about you?"

I tell them, "I don't care. Why do you want to tell me? Do you think I'm going to look at you as a better person or close friend if you tell me something negative about somebody else? Is what you are getting ready to tell me going to make me feel different about that other person? What is your motive in telling me this? I'm not going to let you back a garbage truck into my head!"

I'm assuming you know people out there whose number one aim in life is to say negative things about people and cause controversy. They want to get you distracted by telling you things you have no control over. When it comes down to where the rubber meets the road, the people who love you unconditionally are the only opinions which matter. If people say negative things about you, cut them off. Are you thinking, "Well, I'm going to miss my family and friends?" I have close family and friends who have known me all my life. I share with them a legit business, and they tell me they are not interested without even looking at it.

They then call me on some scam gifting thing a week later, "Hey, Robert, you have to check this out. You put $500 in, and you get 3-5 friends who put in $500, and if they all put in 3-5 friends, you get $500. If they do it again, you get $15,000."

I ask them, "What is the product?"

They say, "Making money!"

I tell them, "What you are doing isn't legal."

They angrily tell me, "You are mad because I came in first!"

All I can do is shake my head and move on to building my empire without them.

BUILDING A NEW FAMILY

I had to create a new family, and you are part of my family. People think I have too many friends, but I don't. I want friends from all over the world, and wish to go out and help as many people as I can and make a difference on this planet. I don't care what people think. I believe in what I am doing.

I recently made some huge moves in my career. I talked to people, and they wanted to give me advice like, "What is so and so going to think?"

I pointed out to them, "Are they going to pay my bills? Are they going to show up to Robert Hollis's life celebration when I am no longer here?"

You must make it a priority to not care about what other people think or say about you. You have to forgive them and forget it. When you forgive people, it doesn't condone what they did. My forgiving someone doesn't make them right; it makes me free. The person who gives most is the one who wins. Focus on giving. Don't focus on thinking about what others think about you.

If you are a know it all, right fighter, "ask hole," are comfortable or a people pleaser, your timing is not correct. You must understand this.

YOU ARE A WINNER

One more group; which is likely you because you are reading this book, is the winners. Look for winners at the right time and place. Build a relationship with many people, because you will find people at the wrong time in their life. Be patient with them, over-deliver, and keep doing it because you are a winner.

Always focus on the fact you will find people who wish to change their lives. Do not spend time with people who are in the wrong place at the wrong time. You've been a winner in the past because you ended up where you needed to be. Because you received your driver's license, you became a winner. If you graduated from high school or college, you have another win. If you are an excellent parent or spouse, you are a winner.

You must believe you are a winner and continue to work on yourself. Don't beat yourself up if you aren't in production but be smart enough to know the steps you have to take to be a winner again. What do you need to do to be a winner as an entrepreneur? What do you need to do to be a winner at_____? You can fill in the blank for your life. It takes action and results to be a winner. You can be a winner if you make a little bit of money or a lot of money. You can be a winner if you can edify and promote a mentor.

THANK -YOU SEAN!

Do you consider the person who introduced me to becoming an entrepreneur a winner? Sean Hennigan didn't make any money, but Sean is a winner to me. He had bravery and used the system. He put me in front of a mentor he edified correctly and promoted. The ripple effect Sean gets for taking and putting me in front of the right mentor at the right time is priceless! Wow! Millions of peoples' lives have changed because he decided to be the right person at the right time and a winner.

You can be a winner, but you must understand you need to work on you. You must get to a point where you have higher expectations, standards, and belief in yourself. If you look at the past years and say, "At least I'm not dead!" Guess what? Your timing is not right! Until you are disgusted with your current situation, nothing is going to happen.

I pray and agree with you, in His name, your timing becomes soon if not NOW.

God loves you, I love you, and pray for your success daily!

Questions for Reflection:

*Which group of people in this chapter do you most relate to?

*Who do you surround yourself with? Do these people encourage and lift you up?

*Who is a Darth Vader in your life?

*What is your focus in life? Do you feel like you are a winner?

CHAPTER FIVE

ALL THINGS ARE POSSIBLE!

"But Jesus looked at them and said, with man this is impossible, but with God all things are possible."

Matthew 19:26

Y ou flat out can do this thing called life! We all have a scorecard. When you look at your life, have you been able to achieve everything you want? Do you say, "I'm far away from where I want to be? I thought I would be there by now, but I don't know why this isn't working!" Do you beat yourself up? Imagine if instead of beating yourself up when you make a mistake, you simply say to yourself, "I made an error, but I have learned from it and am getting "gooder and gooder". I want you to think about every word you say from this point on.

At thirteen years of age, bad circumstances separated me from my two biological brothers. I see them occasionally, but we are not close. I recently got off a call with one of my brothers and found out he was still struggling with life.

He said, "Bobby, I don't know what to do."

I told him, "You do know what to do. You can do this."

He complained, "I am depressed and down in the dumps."

I told him, "The reason you don't work on your mindset, your heart space, controlling your emotional state, and finding a way to stay in the positive is that it's easier not to."

IT'S EASIER NOT TO DO

Everything I do, for example: watch inspirational YouTube channels, pray, meditate, and connect with people, you can do. I'm not doing anything that is crazy hard. It's easy to do, but it's also easy not to do.

People regularly ask me, "How do you do this? How do you do this? How do you do this?"

"You just do it! Everyone can do what I do!"

I call ADD, always dealing (with) distractions. Stop it! Stop making excuses! Stop feeling bad about yourself! Stop saying "Things are not easy for me, I'm overwhelmed, and I'm frustrated!"

Come on! You can do this! We use excuses to stop us from going into action. Do you have a job, or did you have one in the past? The second you go to work and punch into the time clock, you can change your thoughts and go into action. If you don't do what you're hired to do, your boss will fire you, so you do what it takes to keep your job! It's funny how you can do it when it comes to a job, but you find it difficult when it comes to your dreams and goals.

DO YOU NEED TO FIRE YOURSELF?

What if you could employ yourself? You can, because you are an entrepreneur. You can also fire yourself just like I did many times. Go to a mirror and look directly into your eyes. Say, "Listen, I fire you. You procrastinate and don't do anything that you say you are going to do. You give people your word, and then you don't follow through. You don't reach out to new people every day, peak their interest, and fill the funnel. You are not getting conversions. You aren't practicing your skills, learning new skills, and mastering those skills to get better results. You aren't following the company's proven simple system. You are not doing it, so you are fired! Get out of here!"

Then turn around, walk out of the bathroom, come back in, and look into your eyes again and say, "Listen, I'm going to give you one more chance. I know that you can succeed because I've seen you do it in the past with paying bills, getting good grades, getting your driver's license. I've seen you do it with controlling your emotions, being kind to people by giving to the needy and volunteering your time and efforts. You are an honest person! Now it's time to get serious about your life. It's time to find a mentor, listen to that mentor, and start with consistent daily baby steps. It's time to follow a proven system.

Another thing I want you to know is I love you. You are a good friend, spouse, and a reputable community leader. You can learn to be a mentor and leader to others. You are "getting gooder and gooder", every single day in every way. If other people can do it, so can you."

You can do everything I teach. Say to yourself, "I'm going to do what it takes this time." How long should you do it? How about until? My mentor, Jim Rohn, said, "Until is an important word. It means you will never give up."

Regardless of your spiritual beliefs, every religious belief says all things are possible, not a few things, or most things are possible. It means all things are possible for those who believe. It doesn't mean all things are possible for those who say I can't do it. It doesn't state all things are possible to those who doubt themselves, don't believe in themselves, and don't love themselves.

I run into people all the time and wish they would record themselves. Someone told me today, "I just joined a company, and I know this isn't going to build fast."

"Shut up! It does build fast for those who believe. It built fast for me. I walked away from my full-time income in less than 45 days."

I hear people say, "I may learn Facebook, but it's a slow way to build. People aren't successful with marketing on Facebook and online."

"Shut up! For people who know what they are doing, believe it works, take action, they have success."

You can do this like every successful person on the planet who wanted to be an entrepreneur or wanted something better in life. You can be like those who wanted to be happy and wanted financial security. Every single person having success now, at one time didn't know how to do it. It's easy for me to be successful at anything. First, I ask for help, and then I seek out people who have already done what I'm looking to do. I'm not interested in going through the school of hard knocks. Some people are proud to say they've gone through this school. Not me.

My daily routine is simple for me. Every day I connect with brand new people, be a servant to them, be a go-giver, and point, guide and direct. All day I find people who have ears to hear.

DECIDE TO BE STUPID

Do you feel you are super intelligent? I pray that you make a conscious decision like I did, and dumb it down. Instead of being smart, be stupid. Follow the proven system that someone else has done that has made them successful. Let go and believe in faith that if it worked for me, it would work for you.

I decided to be stupid by taking the part of my brain that messes up everything by overthinking and get rid of it. Do you over think? Do you do it in relationships? Do you do it in your spiritual life? Have you ever wondered how to improve your spiritual life? I don't want to blow anyone out of the water by saying, "If I spend uninterrupted time in prayer talking to my Creator, He will draw close to me." Some people say, "That is too simple, it's got to be harder than that! I don't know how to pray. There has to be a different way to pray. What do you say when you pray? Is it meditation? Should I do it in the morning or the evening? Should I get down on my knees to pray? Is it okay if I pray in the afternoon? How long should I pray?

Come on, we all do the same stupid stuff in every area of our lives. You cannot build personal relationships and have any closeness in your lives unless you spend time getting to know people. That's all you need to do. Learn to have a conversation and build relationships.

The information I teach is simple. It's worked for twenty-two years before me, and it's now worked the thirty plus years I've been using it. You shouldn't change it or try to make it better. You need to practice the proven system and keep doing it until you find the right people. Find the people who tell you that this sounds simple, makes sense, and they think they can do it. Learn to pay attention, be a student, and be a listener. Learn new things, simple things that work, and duplicate. Don't be a know-it-all.

What I do is simple. I reach out to people by being a go-giver. I peak their interest and say as little to them as possible. The person puts their name and e-mail in, takes a test drive as a pre-enrollee in the company, and he or she watches a video. The system sends them emails to create excitement, enthusiasm, and urgency.

"Whoa, wait a minute Robert! It's getting a little deep for me. Can you back it up a little? It's getting a little challenging. How do you say that again? I'm not sure the sequence that you said to do."

"Are you kidding me?" Just be nice, be a go-giver, and be a friend. Do what you would like people to do to you.

I AM AN ANOMALY

I figured out that I am an anomaly because I am in the top 1% of income earners because I chose to dumb everything down. I made a conscious decision to be stupid. I was so desperate, broke, and bankrupt in every part of my life when I met my mentor. I came to my mentor, and all I was interested in doing was changing my life. Every area in my life sucked big time! I knew I had to trust and believe, get out of my head, and go with my heart and my spirit. I needed to work from an emotional and spiritual level, not an analytical level.

Do you feel you keep trying, and it doesn't work? When are you going to listen to someone like me who says, "Now that you've already proven that you are too smart to be successful, can you make a conscious decision to dumb it down? Decide to be stupid and follow the system. Stop over-thinking!"

WE HAVE IT EASY TODAY!

If I followed you around and watched you, what would I see? Are you talking, chatting, and texting? Would I find you are doing the things I do but with the wrong people saying the wrong words? Would I see you aren't talking to new people, but you are communicating with people you already have talked to over and over again? All I do is share the same story other people tell, but I connect with new people. That's all I do!

We have it easy today! Before the internet, I had to go out around skyscrapers, malls, food courts, and talk and build relationships with a group of strangers. I walked up to them and found a way to start a conversation. Now we have the internet, social media, smartphones, Google hangouts and zooms. I still do the same thing, connect with people. You can do as I do, but the question is, will you do it?

PROVE SUCCESS WRONG

What else are you doing? What are you doing with your free time? Master and learn some new skills where you can be a go-giver and give to a bunch of hurt people making their lives better. Try to prove all the best writings and success gurus wrong for example, *what you give you get*. When the farmer gives, he gets. According to Deuteronomy 28:8, "The Lord will send a blessing on your barns and on everything you put your hand to. The Lord will bless you in the land." Napoleon Hill of *Think and Grow Rich* says, "If you help enough people get what they want in life, you will get what you want out of life." Why not prove it?

Do you believe everything people tell you? You need to find out where your thoughts originated. How do you know that what you feel is correct? Think about the words which come out of your mouth, good or bad. What if someone asked you to prove everything you said was true?

I used to believe the myth that if you wanted to make six figures, for example, $200,000 or $300,000, you needed to go to college. I don't believe this anymore, because I and many others have proven it wrong. If you believed something and never took the time to check it out to see if it's true, you are spreading lies. Let's say you think something but didn't take the time to see if it's true because you believe it's 100% true. When you share with energy, passion, and enthusiasm, you come across as more believable than the person who is lying, but you didn't take the time to check its truthfulness. In my mid

20's, I started asking myself how do I know that's true? I questioned everything.

My mom and my foster moms used to say, "Bobby, be sure you put on a jacket because if you go out in the cold, you will get the flu or catch a cold." That's not true. You don't get a virus by being out in the cold; you get a virus from someone who spreads the virus. What untrue statements do you make?

PLEASE GET OFF THE KOOL-AID

You don't have to exaggerate, concoct facts, or drink the Kool-Aid. How many undocumented people do you follow? Have you followed their teachings but haven't gotten any results because it worked in the past but not now? It's like me telling you that you need to get a pager and use it for your business. We used to use these successfully in business but not anymore. You must be careful that the information and mentor you follow have current documentation of success. You need to lead by example and reach out to people who aren't afraid to show you their documentation. Find someone who teaches other people how to make a full-time income. Also, find others who are willing to say that this mentor helped them.

QUESTION EVERYTHING

Stop listening to people who are full of crap and undocumented people. Question everything you see and hear and ask, "How do I know that it's true?" Do you believe you get the truth from the media, internet, television, and radio? It's your job to question everything that you see. Question it before you share it with others as truth.

I want to believe the best in people, don't you? My mentor asked me when I started working with him, "Robert, do you know what the Golden Rule is?"

I said, "Of Course! Do unto others as you would have them do unto you."

"No, it's not Robert! The Golden rule is the person who makes the gold, makes the rules." I want to believe my definition of the Golden Rule, but I've learned I need to question what I hear.

TAKE PERSONAL RESPONSIBILITY

Can you be responsible for all the "fricken" decisions you make all year? Can you take personal responsibility and say, "Enough is enough! I'm disgusted?" It would be different if I asked you to dunk a basketball. I'm not asking you to dunk a basketball. I'm not asking you to play the piano. I'm not asking you to dance the cha-cha. I'm not asking you to lift a car or run a marathon. I'm asking you to connect with people, serve others, learn to build relationships, and be a go-giver. You can do this!

God created you to be great, happy, to love and be loved, to be joyful, and to share the joy, which is easy to do, but you choose not to do it. Why? The crazy thing about people is that when it seems too easy, they do nothing. I've mentioned I do nothing you can't do. People say I'm more animated then they are. Yes, I may be more animated, but you should have seen me when I first became an entrepreneur. People say I talk well. You should have seen me when I first started.

You can do this! I need you to repeat over and over again you know you can do this! It is simple and easy!

Are you thinking, "I know **you** can do this, but you don't have a clue who I used to be." Every excuse you have, I can find someone who had the same one and became successful. Everything which stops us from our dreams and goals in life begins with thinking. It's amazing how easy everything is if you just do it! You know what to do and how to do it. Make from today on your best year ever! You deserve to have a better life, and it starts today.

God loves you, I love you, and pray for your success daily!

Questions for Reflection:

*Do you need to fire yourself and then rehire yourself?

*Are you willing to dumb it down and decide to be stupid?

*What is one thing you say all the time which maybe isn't true?

*What are you doing in your life that worked in the past but isn't working now?

CHAPTER SIX

WOW! THAT WAS EASY!

"Be kind and compassionate to one another, forgiving each other, just as in Christ, God forgave you."

Ephesians 4:32

Write down the things you believe are your strengths. The reason I want you to write what you are best at is that you become best at it by first deciding. When you choose you say, "I believe I can do it!" You also think, "Wow! That was easy!"

Some of us procrastinate, and I do it too. Procrastination is suicide on the installment plan. Do you have ADD (always dealing with distractions)? You need to have a "richual" of being productive instead of just being active. An idea to help you be more productive: set alarms on your phone every fifteen minutes. Don't forget to hit the snooze button to keep you on track.

THE "WHAT IF WORLD"

We worry even though we know most worrying never happens anyway. We live in a "what if" world. What if this happens and what if that happens? What if it doesn't work?" Well, what if it does work? People say "well, what if..." I say, "What if we get hit by an asteroid, and we are all gone? If you want to play in the "what if" world, there's an example of the "what if" world."

Think about the things you wrote down which you excel in. Maybe you don't feel you are good at many things but think about it. Do you consider yourself a good parent, a good spouse, or a good friend? You have the talents you have because you first decided. Once you made the decision, you committed. The rest comes easy.

Are you struggling right now? If you are stuck, I don't think you have made the decision. You are also not committed to taking action needed to reach your goals. I have done many things in my life which are extremely painful and even extremely difficult. I didn't care because I decided and committed to becoming an entrepreneur.

YOU MUST MAKE A COMMITMENT

I know millions of people on the planet dissatisfied with one or more areas of their lives. They want something, and they want it bad. They pray or meditate daily for you or me to find them. Do you feel reaching out to people is difficult? Do you think going out and talking to people is difficult? In my mind, if it's hard, you haven't decided.

In my early 20's, I became not only a black belt in taekwondo; I became a bodyguard. I weighed 168 pounds and benched over 352 pounds. I participated in the martial arts studio four days a week, and three days a week I worked out at the gym. I was serious! I decided, and nothing stopped me. People said in disbelief, "I can't believe you practice that hard in martial arts."

I told them, "It's easy. It's fun, and I love martial arts! I want to be a black belt and a professional fighter." I achieved my goals.

Many people told me they could never do martial arts. How many couples look at people who are already parents and say they could never be a parent. Once they decide to start their family, they commit to figuring it out, and nothing gets in their way. How about marriage? Suddenly, everyone around you is married. You say, "I don't know if I could do this, what if this happens, or what if that happens?" Suddenly, you decide to get married, because you find the right person, and you say, "Will you marry me?" You make plans and get married and say, "I do." Wow! That was easy! Once you make the commitment whatever happens and whatever you do will become natural.

There have been many difficult things in my life; they seemed difficult because I hadn't made the decision and commitment to figure them out. Once I had the right attitude, it all came together. Do you ever get anxiety because you feel you might mess something up or fail at something? Wow! The way we talk to ourselves is ridiculous! Isn't it? All it takes is a decision to face the fear and figure it out.

STOP TRYING, START DOING

Look at one of the things you are above average at and understand you had first to decide and believe you could do it. You did it and declared, "Wow! That was easy!" You can be happy, be anything you want to be, change your mind, and change your thoughts. It's easy!

If you struggle, whine, and complain, I don't believe you have made a full decision and a commitment to change. You are doing what Yoda would beat you up at, *"Stop trying. Start doing!"*

I know you can do it. The critical point is I want **you** to believe you can do it. Will you do it? Most people died in their twenties, but they aren't buried yet. Wow! Every day they are bored, depressed, and say things aren't going well for them. Woe is them! Make sure this isn't you! Believe you can do it, decide to do it, and commit to doing it. It's easy to do and don't forget, easy not to do. It's your choice.

God loves you, I love you, and pray for your success daily!

<u>Questions for Reflection:</u>

*List five things that you feel you are best at.

*What areas in your life do you procrastinate?

*Where in your life are you living in the "what if" world?

*How committed are you to reaching your goals?

CHAPTER SEVEN

BELIEF- HOW TO GET IT AND KEEP IT!

"But those who hope in the Lord will renew their strength. They will soar on wings like eagles; they will run and not grow weary. They will walk and not faint."

Isaiah 40:31

I want you to think about this idea. If every day you get up, choose not to go into action, don't apply the knowledge you learned, you aren't going to get the results you want. When you don't get the results, it tears down your belief and confidence. When it tears down your faith and trust, whatever you are marketing, you won't share and promote it. You aren't going to have the most important thing you see in many of the successful people on the planet...belief.

What do you believe in? What is something if somebody tried to cross you a little bit you would fight them on it? "If you don't believe in something, you will fall for anything." Is the belief you have strong enough if someone tried to confront you with it, your hair w stand on the back of your neck; you would get tough and hold your ground? Think about that. If you are a mom and someone says something about your kids or does something to your kids, will the Momma Bear come out? Would you say, "You can trash my husband or me, but you talk badly about my kids, I'm going to go off on you and take you out!"

WHERE BELIEF COMES FROM

I want you to honestly think about the ideas which cause you to have a strong, above average, belief. Go ahead and write them down. One of the things I want you to ask yourself is where did that belief come? I want to point out you have it in you. Your dreams, visions, love, connection, contribution, and passion are still in you, stronger than they've ever been. You must learn to tap into them and use them. Are you listening to me? They are still there.

Suddenly something happens which excites you. People might look at you and think, "Who is that person? I haven't seen that kind of laughter and excitement in a long time." You have joy inside you. You have all the positive characteristics that have been waiting for you. Have you heard the phrase, "If you don't use it, you will lose it?" Let me share something that should cause you to be "jac¹⁻   t of your mind" about. You still have these   acteristics in you, and all you must do is

            le have a belief in marriage, in
            even in the kind of car they drive. They
            y. Chevys are best!"

64

Where do you find belief? First, look to see if you ever had confidence in yourself. I know beyond any doubt that you had it. You must find a significant emotional event in your life where your joy, enthusiasm, faith, and belief showed up.

It's fun talking to children. You ask them, "What are you going to be when you grow up?"

The little boy says, "I'm going to be a fireman!"

You ask the little boy, "Are you sure?"

He enthusiastically says, "Yes, I am!"

Another child says, "I want to be a singer and an actress." Another child says, "I want to be a gymnast."

Every one of these children believes they will reach their dreams, and no one can convince them any differently. We as adults still have our inner child in us. Point one is you still have it, point two you had it in the past, and now you need to find it again. Where do you find faith, belief, and this magic stuff? You hang around people who have it.

Let's talk about laughter and joy. You get around a bunch of friends who are having fun and laughing; suddenly, it's contagious. You find yourself laughing just because your friends are. Many people recognize me because of my funny laugh. Laughter has power and improves the quality of our lives. Every day I find ways to bring joy and laughter into my life and the lives of those around me. Focus on bringing laughter into your world.

Have you ever watched a video on YouTube where you see a guy with headphones sitting by himself on a subway, intently staring at his smartphone and laughing hysterically? A couple of other people begin laughing only because this guy is, and then more people start laughing. Suddenly, everyone is laughing hysterically, but no one except the first guy has a clue why they are laughing.

FIND PEOPLE DOING WHAT YOU WANT TO DO

You must get around people who believe 1000% in what they are doing and get connected to them. You need to find the people who have successfully done what you want to do. If you're going to learn how to dance, you might want to take lessons from a dance instructor who has won the "Dancing with the Stars" ball three times. He's purchased a studio where he gives lessons and has helped many people learn to dance. This instructor's belief in the fact that you can dance will carry you through all your self-limiting beliefs as you train.

You could say to him, "I don't think I can do it. I have two left feet. I don't have any rhythm. I'm lazy. I'm overweight. I have a bum knee."

He will say "I don't care, I can teach you. I have faith and belief that you can dance. I have learned to dance, and others have, so can you."

If you run into people who have already done what you want to do, they can help you. They have a belief and have never forgotten who they used to be. I remember having no money. I remember not knowing anything about marketing. I remember being scared to death. Let's pause and think about the statement "scared to death". That's a bold statement when I'm talking about connecting with somebody, doing a presentation, and handling objections.

Are you kidding me? Have you ever utt

From this point on, think about every w

BELIEF IS STRONGER THAN FEAR

Where did I learn to get over my fear
who not only believed they could build a group, but they
knew they could do it fast. I watched them do it. My
mentor had a belief like the dance instructor example, and
he could convey it to others. Confidence pulls people
through. I believe you can do it. Come on you aren't going
to get hurt! Go ahead jump off into the water. It's going to
be great! No problem! I am here for you.

You have another person who says, "I wouldn't do it,
in fact, I haven't done it. You might get hurt! You better be
careful! Are you 100% sure you want to do this?" Does
that person seem familiar? That person is you. You aren't
saying this in actual words, but your lack of belief in
yourself speaks louder than any words you could ever say.
Did you catch that?

THE SECRET TO GOLF

Let's say you take your friend out to play golf and this
is his first-time golfing. He's never even held a golf club.
Your friend can believe he knows how to golf, realize that
other people are good at golf, but when he gets there, it
doesn't go well. He didn't take the time to find a mentor,
coach, or trainer to teach him the necessary things to do
to be a successful golfer. It doesn't matter how hard he
swings the golf club or how many times he swings it. If he
doesn't have the right information, he isn't going to get the
correct results. If he doesn't get the proper education and

...cs on being successful, he will walk away mad. Later in life, someone will step up to him and say, "Hey listen, we should play golf."

Your friend isn't interested and says, "I already tried golfing. It's not for me, and it doesn't work."

That isn't true, but this is your friend's belief because he didn't have someone teach him all he needed to know. Does this sound familiar?

HOW MAGIC HAPPENED

What if you believed in a system and the person running the system? When you think it can be done and others have done the system with success, you will say, "If they can do it, I can do it." They believe in their abilities to do it, so that's where the magic starts. My POP (point of passion) happened when Sean introduced me to entrepreneurship. He never made any money in marketing, but he met a guy, Bill Gouldd, who instilled belief in him. Sean had faith and hope, and I felt his excitement when he approached me. It's worth taking note of this.

Some people have a lack of belief in what they have, lack of confidence in what they do, and they don't hang around people who have faith and hope in their lives. Their lack of understanding is crushing them. It's a struggle for them every day. It's frustrating because they don't have the success they desire; they don't have confidence in the system or process. They most importantly don't have faith and belief in the person leading them.

Always Remember:

1. You had belief in the past.
2. You can get it again.
3. How you keep belief is knowing how you found it.

MY MORNING "RICH UAL"

Every day I need to refuel my belief. I do this by getting up early every morning, being incredibly grateful, and doing my morning "rich-ual". I start my day with gratitude time, prayer time, and my personal development time where I listen to my mentors. Every year as part of my personal growth, I find a new leader to follow, but my lifelong mentors are Roger Penske, Bill Gouldd, Jim Rohn, Bob Proctor, and Wallace Wattles. Once I have my mind in the right place, I go through all my messages, but this never comes before my gratitude, prayer, and personal growth time. An attitude of gratitude is essential to any lasting success.

You must act and hang around those who have belief, faith and are plugged-in. If you don't have excitement and stay plugged-in, your trust and confidence will fade away. Don't whine, complain, cry, and expect someone to pump you up. It's up to you.

YOU BECOME WHO YOU HANG AROUND

The worse thing is finding people who give up, lose their belief and faith, and now they wait for you to pull them back up. They are saying, "Can you please resell me on me?"

I want to give hundreds of millions of dollars to charity. Why? I want to give because I hung around people who did it. Now I'm seeing people in the billionaire league who give 30 million dollars.

Do you say, "I don't even know how I'm going to pay my rent this month?" Really, could you play a little smaller in this game called life? You become who you hang around. Let's all sit around the house and watch some Jerry Springer episodes. Let's spend time viewing some Dr. Phil and see him beat up on people. Are you kidding me?

The reason many people aren't successful and the winners they can be is simple. Have you heard the statement, "You become who you hang around?" Winners hang around other winners. Winners don't hang around posers, wannabes, whiners, and amateurs. Start hanging around people who believe in you.

Let me give you a simple example. As you go through elementary school, your parents, grandparents, kids you hang around and everyone around you, expect you to go to fifth grade. They want you to go to sixth grade, junior high, and high school. The people surrounding you believe and hope you do what everybody else is doing. Do you usually follow along with others' plans for you? I call that being a "sheeple."

In my environment and where I grew up, no one expected me to go to college. I had made incredible money by the time I became a junior in high school. Many people told me if I was going to make money at a job, I needed to go out and be a mechanic, plumber, electrician, or a construction worker in the oil field. I realized I could do that without a college degree. Because my aunts, uncles, and cousins believed the same way, I followed them. Now, what did everyone expect me to do? They hoped I would get married, have kids, keep my job, and be a responsible citizen. That's it! I reached all the expectations everyone put on me!

Do you currently feel stuck and wonder why you aren't doing anything with your life? I promise you it's because you are hanging around a group of people who don't expect anything out of you.

ASSOCIATION WITH PEERS

Let me give you one more example. Let's say you set out on an incredible trip with four of your favorite friends. One of the days you go to this beautiful ocean. You walk up to an inlet where people are jumping off a cliff into the beautiful blue sea below. You curiously watch as these strangers jump off the cliff. You see young people, old people, and people from different races who live in different countries. The cliff is high enough where you don't feel comfortable jumping, but you continue watching as everyone goes crazy jumping into the water. A person your age notices you are standing next to the cliff and says to you, "I did it! You can do it! Come on!"

You excitedly go to your group of friends. One of your friends says, "I'm not doing it! Are you stupid?" Another friend says, "People get hurt. What if something happens to you?" Another one says, "You are crazy if you jump off that cliff!" The last friend you came with tries the reverse peer pressure and says, "I wouldn't do it! Please don't do it! You're scaring me! I've heard of people dying who have jumped off cliffs!"

Suddenly, because of peer pressure, you don't do the things you would love to do and make you excited. You don't do the things which would take your breath away, would take you from existing to living, so you stay average. I hang around a different group of people. My sons, my family, and the people I hang around are the opposite. They would make me jump off the cliff. They would jump before me.

Now, let's imagine you hang around a whole new group of people. You walk up to the cliff, and one of your friends say, "This is going to be awesome!" He jumps without even hesitating, and your next friend jumps. One by one your other two friends jump. You approach the edge of the cliff, and as you look down, you realize no-one got hurt. Everyone cheers you on saying, "Come on! Come on! If we can do it, you can do it!" You excitedly decide to jump because of your peers.

Start hanging around a group of people who have a high standard for their lives and expect you to have a high standard for your life as well. They coach and mentor you and say, "If I can do it, you can too!" You want to hang around people who say, "Hey, we are all going to Spain. We are all going to Brazil. We are all going to London. Let's go!" You want to hang around people who expect more out of you. They want you to drive nice cars. They require you to live a higher level of life. Hang around a group of people who demand you to better yourself, give more money to charity, travel the world, and look for you to be a winner.

I used to be a gigantic fish in a small pond. What does that mean? I worked on professional race cars. I made

$50,000 a year, and everyone around me made much less than me. I was comfortable, complacent, and an influential person. Guess what happened? Sean introduced me to a guy, Bill Gouldd, who made $62,000 a month. Not only that; but Bill also had taught people to make ten to fifteen thousand a month. I started hanging around them and became an extremely small fish in a vast pond. Suddenly, I had to raise my standards because they expected more of me. I could no longer be complacent and had to get out of my comfort zone. Bill encouraged me and told me that I could do it. That's how I came to where I am today. Mentors can make an enormous difference in your life and help you become a winner.

STAY PLUGGED IN

You need to have faith and belief. You must build trust and stay plugged-in. Are you a yo-yo, up one day and down the other? If you are, you better find a way to stay plugged in more than you ever have. The reason I'm passionate is that I plugged into a system my mentor taught me. I did everything he told me to do because I was in desperation mode. I made over $258,000 my first year. I didn't yet have the faith or belief, but I knew who did. I plugged into him all day every day. I watched his videotapes and audios repeatedly which built up my confidence. When I built my understanding, I could easily talk to people and build relationships with them. I would grab them and put them in front of the person who had the most belief, Bill. He did all the things I knew I could have done but for some reason, the people believed him, and he inspired them to act. I didn't make myself the deal.

My success came because I listened to my mentor, built my faith and belief up, edified my mentor, and got my people in front of him. He took over and got the people jacked up, and they joined. Promoting my mentor is how I earned checks. I also received rank advancements, recognition, and travel opportunities. I never had to work for anyone again. What a concept!

Don't ever forget you have everything you need to be successful, but you must stay plugged in with the people who believe in you, promote you, and have faith in you. Doing anything without belief is a lost cause.

God loves you, I love you, and pray for your success daily!

Questions for Reflection:

*Is your belief stronger than your fears?

*What is your daily "rich-ual"?

*What is something if somebody tried to cross you a little bit, you would fight them on it?

*Are you hanging around a group of people who expect a higher standard of life for you?

-CHAPTER EIGHT-

DO YOU BELIEVE YOU ARE FREE?

"You have stayed long enough at this mountain. (It's time for you to move on and experience God's favor)."

Deuteronomy 1:6

Do you have your definitions for faith, wealth, and success? What is your definition of freedom and what does it mean to you? My definition of freedom is to have choices. It allows me on a day to day basis to do all I love with the people I want to do it with. Freedom allows me to decide to do anything I want with my family and not have anyone but me in control of my schedule.

Most importantly, having the money to do everything I want, that's real freedom for me. The reason people don't build and go for their dreams and goals is that they don't envision the pleasure in their minds ahead of reaching their dreams. I have been able to see the happiness.

WINNING THE LOTTERY

Imagine you won the lottery and it gave you freedom. How would your life be different? Would you continue to do everything you are doing right now? What would you do differently on a day to day basis if money and time weren't the issues? How many people dream about winning the lottery but never go out and buy a lottery ticket? It's effortless and straightforward to go to the store and buy a lottery ticket, right? Why do the majority of the people say statements such as the odds are too much, that's stupid, I'm not going to waste my money, and I'm tired?" They get into excuseitus and brokeitus because they are poor in their thoughts. They think that it will take too much thought to walk or drive to the store and pay a couple of dollars for a ticket. They say, "They rigged this. I'm not lucky. Winning the lottery only happens to other people."

It's hard to have the winning ticket if you don't buy one. The last lottery recently paid out 3.2 billion dollars. Everyone who didn't buy a ticket, including me, made up an excuse why they didn't buy. Its mind boggling to me that the people who didn't get a ticket get upset with the people who win the lottery.

I mention the lottery example because people do still have hopes and dreams that can inspire them to act. People have money for lottery tickets, so please quit telling me no one has any money, or everyone they know is lazy. Well some of them got off their ass and bought a ticket. Another lie is people don't dream anymore. Are you kidding me? People wrote lists of things they dreamed of buying before they even bought the tickets. The lottery gave me hope and inspired me because it shows me not all people in America are dead.

THE ROAD TO FREEDOM

Are you good at lying to yourself? Do you convince yourself you are free even though you are not? Do you tell yourself you are okay, comfortable, things are not bad, well at least not as bad as people in other countries? Do you continually make up excuses because you are supposed to be grateful for all you have?

Take time and imagine your perfect day. My ideal day is to be there for my family whenever they need me, and continuously help more people each day get all they want in life. You must have the idea of your perfect day which lights you up and makes you jacked out of your mind every day.

Go back to your definition of freedom. If your definition is the same as mine, but someone tells you when you must pay a bill, that's stress, not freedom. Do you have a mortgage due at the beginning of the month and a car payment at the end of the month? Do you have credit card payments due every month where you only pay the minimum due? Do you have pressure you shouldn't have? How can you get rid of the stress? Freedom comes in not owing anything to anybody. That's why it's called debt free. Imagine conquering your debt. Imagine not having any more student loan debt? How do you feel? It's crucial!

I'm not saying to quit your job. I realize we need to be responsible and some people must have jobs. Do you have someone telling you when you have to be at work? Do you have someone saying you can go to lunch and how long lunch you can take? Do you have someone telling you whether you can take a weekend off or a week off? Do you have someone say whether you can stay at home with your sick child or not? Do you believe you are free? Take time to understand and work towards a different level of freedom for you.

THE PRICE OF FREEDOM

Everyone has their definition of freedom. Even though I'm not a billionaire or haven't made a hundred million dollars, I understand my definition of freedom. I have taken the time to understand marketing to have freedom. I take the time to build a loyal, satisfied customer base. I have learned the principles of residual income and leverage. I teach other people to succeed which gives me a percentage for education and teaching of others. I understand the amount of money I make residually would be the same as having fifty or sixty million dollars in the bank. I call this true freedom!

Are you able to be free to give to others whenever you want? When someone needs your help if you don't have the time and financial ability to help them, are you free? I want to get serious with you for a moment. Please listen, pay attention, and let it absorb in. Don't think I'm beating you up. Many people out there have fought for your freedom and your ability to become an entrepreneur. If you don't take advantage of it and don't become free, was their price of freedom worth nothing? If you don't take advantage of it, freedom doesn't exist for you.

You live someplace where you can become an entrepreneur, find an excellent product or service, and can market it to become free. You can do all you like to do, when you want to do it, with those you love, and help others learn to do this too. You can give freely. Freedom is available. Are you taking advantage of it?

When I understood the principles of *Science of Getting Rich* by Wallace Wattles and understood the principles of *Think and Grow Rich*, I realized how blessed I was. I was unstoppable! Do you believe you are invincible and blessed? Do you think you are a winner? J.D Rockefeller said, "I'd rather get 1% of 100 people's efforts than 100% of my own." You must go out and learn something new, invest money, and take time to make yourself better. If you don't, then shame on you! If you blow this freedom away watching mindless TV, shame on you! First, you need to invest in you. Stop spending money on stupid stuff, save the money, invest in you, and take the time to learn something you can teach somebody else. Once I found a mentor, I spent all my time and money into learning. As I learned, I put people in front of my mentor at the same time to leverage my time.

RAISE YOUR EXPECTATIONS

You owe it to yourself to become a better person, have better communication, and raise your expectations. Are you happy with your life? Are you doing the same things this year you did the previous year which didn't work? The first step is to invest in you because you deserve it. The second step is to build strong relationships and be above average.

Stop making excuses for not having freedom because it's available everywhere in the world. Stop it! You are surrounded by people who are still in a *stinking thinking* mentality. The worst thing that can happen is people know a way out, but they choose not to take it. In other words, they know freedom is available, and they decide not to be free. Wow!

Are you a decisive person and believe you will be free? Are you committed to doing everything you want with whom you wish? As you are reading this, it is your year! You need to start your year today. J Paul Getty said, "It's easy to become successful because no one else is trying." We live in a world right now where most everybody tells us why they shouldn't do something outside the box. They ask," Why should I work harder than anybody else?" Again, I call these people "sheeples."

I hope you can get some cause behind you to stop being average and get rid of your excuses! Some people say they deal with mental clutter on an emotional level. You must grow up! Find a mentor, invest your time and money, master the mundane, find something you can market which changes people's lives, and spend all day every day advancing towards your freedom. Do it because other people believed it was worth it and gave their lives. Do it because other people lost the people they loved for our freedom. Do it for them if you can't do it for yourself. Do it for your kids or all the people you love. As you go through your day, remember that the big things you do are important, but you will be recognized based on mastering the mundane.

Please stop making excuses! Do all you need to do to be able to share. Go out and teach people the information you're learning to become an entrepreneur, a marketer, an online marketer... Learn the goals of reciprocity and show the world you can become one of the people who accomplished everything you set out to do.

PLAYING SMALL DOES NO ONE ANY FAVORS

We live in a world today where people attempt to be politically correct about everything. They don't want to hurt anybody's feelings. They think everyone needs to love them. Love them for what? Love them for being professional, average, procrastinator, excuse makers? Should we tell them we are proud of them and give them an award because they came into a business opportunity and hung around mentors worth millions of dollars who sacrificed their time and money learning from other millionaires? Should we award them for playing small? I have tried to give people this information, and they go out and find something better to do every day. They waste their time, instead of spending it learning, applying, and sharing their knowledge for the other person to be free.

Being successful and leading people to a better way of life, you will become the person you know you are; the person you've always wanted to become. Be the person who God created you to be, great! It's time to make the decision and be committed to living great where being average is a thing of the past. Get disgusted with where you are and do more. Say to yourself, "I can do more, I will do more, and be more." The most important thing is to believe you can be free. Be great! Be a winner!

God loves you, I love you, and pray for your success daily!

Questions for Reflection:

*What is your definition of freedom?

*What is your perfect day?

*Do you believe you are free? How can you change to be free?

*Do you think you are unstoppable and blessed?

CHAPTER NINE

DO YOU KNOW WHAT YOU WANT?

"But when you ask, you must believe and not doubt, because the one who doubts is like a wave of the sea, blown and tossed by the wind."

James 1:6

Do you genuinely know what you want in life? My involvement with many companies shows each company has a couple of groups in common. The first group is people who have gotten in who have made hundreds of thousands and even millions of dollars. Another group of people never did anything, so they never made a dime. Why does the first group have success and the other group doesn't? The first group of leaders knows what they want.

I can help anybody get want they want in life. I have a hard time finding people who know what they want. Do you know what you want? If you don't know where you are going, it really doesn't matter which path you take. My question to you is if you don't know where you are going, how will you know when you get there?

You say, "I want money."

"Good, that's easy! Here's a dollar and now you have more money."

You say, "I want freedom. I want to travel. I want to lose weight. I want to be smarter. I want to learn how to play a musical instrument. I want to learn how to swim."

We all want to do many things. When people know what they want in life, it's incredible the passion, the persistence, and consistency that they have in achieving what they want. Persistence and consistency are the keys to ongoing success. The winner of the race is the one who realizes that today is only one more rung on the ladder towards his or her goal.

The truth and reason people don't have all they want is they genuinely don't want it bad enough. Look back throughout your life and think about times in your life where you wanted something, really wanted it. You wanted a driver's license. You wanted to drive a car. You wanted to finish school. You wanted a pair of shoes. You wanted a job. You wanted a relationship. You wanted children. You wanted an apartment. When you look throughout your life, things you truly wanted you did everything you needed to do to get them. You couldn't get them off your mind. You received what you wanted because you became one hundred percent focused.

Different areas like financial, family, career, physical, spiritual, and mental make up your life. You have all these areas in your life where you want things to be better. Take time and write down what you want from each of these different areas of your life.

I DON'T WANT IT BAD ENOUGH

I make excuses because I'm as human as everyone else. Until recently I was right around 290 pounds which made me easily 100 pounds overweight. Listen closely now! I wanted to lose weight as you want to change your life in some way. I 100% wanted to lose weight, but I didn't want it bad enough. You know how you can tell? I didn't do the things every day I was supposed to be doing to lose 100 pounds and get in better shape. I wasn't eating as healthy as I should. I wasn't drinking enough water. I wasn't exercising twenty minutes a day. I wasn't listening to audios which dealt with my mentality on losing weight. I wasn't doing the things I was supposed to be doing.

Was it easy to drink water? Was it easy to listen to audios? Was it easy to eat healthier? It was easy, but it was easier not to. When people saw me and saw I was overweight, they thought, "I have to get Robert on my weight loss product, if Robert knew about my product, If Robert knew about my company, Look, Robert, look!" Listen I don't want to burst people's bubble, but I wasn't going to take advantage of any one of those products because I said I wanted to lose weight, but the fact is I didn't want it bad enough. If you're involved in one home-based business after another and one company after company after another and personal growth after another, you are doing what makes you feel good. You say you want to be better financially, but do you honestly want it?

People say, "You don't know me!" Yes, I do! I'm the one who owned an expensive elliptical. I had weights and a Bow Flex. I had all kinds of things around the house, but all I would have needed was a couple of water jugs, and if I moved my butt every day, I would have seen results.

All this makes us feel good because now we don't have to look in the mirror and say, "I am not trying." We try to convince ourselves we are trying by saying, "Yes, I am, I finished the mentorship program. I learned from this training. Don't you remember, I drove to that other training? I bought that book and these other books. I got involved in a few companies."

You need to write in your journal everything you want. You must find something you want badly enough that it keeps you up at night. There have been times when I wanted things in my life. I became super focused on them, and it kept me awake at night. Do you say you want money? Do you realize you need to pique the interest to as many people as you can and say as little as possible? You have to build relationships online and offline and take the time to help them. If you tell yourself, "I'm not sure I'm ready to talk to people." You will wake up every day and not contact people. You won't build relationships, and you won't form a group of people. You say you want to, but, honestly do you?

FIGURE OUT HOW TO DO IT AND DO IT FAST!

What is a real want? There have been times when I didn't want the landlord to kick me out of my apartment. See I didn't want to live in the street. When I didn't want to live in the street, it's amazing how focused I got, and how I built up my courage and posture. I did all I needed to do and asked people if they could help me out. When I didn't want to be in the street, and I wanted to stay in my apartment, it's amazing how I found a way. When I didn't want my lights shut off, I found a way to keep them on. When I asked you, "What do you want?" Are you still struggling to figure it out? Again, let me reiterate this statement, I can help you get what you want. You need to know what you want and be willing to do what it takes to get it. When you say I want a new house, or I'd like a nicer car or to pay down debt, it's easy to do what I do. Drinking water is easy. Walking is easy. Not taking seconds is easy. Jim Rohn says it best, "It's easy to do but easier not to do."

Unfortunately, we don't do it. I can tell if you wanted something bad enough, you would have already had it. There's a statement which says everything takes time. Do you know it to be true? I needed to make $10,000 super-fast, and if I didn't, I would be out on the street. I figured out how to do it quickly. If you still struggle with deciding what you want in your life, figure out everything you don't want anymore in your life. I don't want to have my electricity shut off. I don't want my car repossessed. I don't want to live here anymore. I don't want to have the long commute to work anymore. I don't want that job anymore. I don't want people telling me what to do. I don't want to make any more excuses. I don't want to break my promises.

If you look at your life, all the way up to this point, do you have everything that you desire and deserve? Do you have everything that you need, and everything that you want to make you happy? If you don't, it's because you have become distracted or allowed excuses to continue to sabotage your success, your happiness, your state of passion, your enthusiasm, and living every moment of your life like it's the best moment of your life.

You must be clear on your wants and needs. Don't forget to write your thoughts in your journal. It helps to put it on a dream board or make a video or both. Watch or look at your wants every day, get emotional about all you want, and believe you can have them. When you do, you will start doing the things you aren't doing now, and you're going to become successful.

FOCUS ON WHAT MATTERS

You already know what you need to do. We all at some point say we don't know what to do or say, which is an excuse not to do it. "I wish I knew more about the product. I wish I knew more about the pay plan. I wish I knew more." No, you don't need to know more, you want to get results. Start focusing on the things which matter.

Let's say suddenly you get sick or hurt. You now don't want to be sick anymore. You want to be well, have energy, and feel healthy and alive. Your body hurts. You don't want your back pain anymore. You don't want your knee to hurt. You want to be pain-free. When things get bad enough, suddenly your whole life wraps around making sure the pain is gone. You take the action steps you need to get well.

For all the people who don't want something bad enough, the world is selling you shortcuts. You have a cold, and you go to the doctor. He tells you to rest and drink plenty of fluids, and in one week you should feel better. You decide to take a shortcut by taking all the cold medicines and Nyquil for rest. None of this works. You finally decide you need to rest and drink plenty of fluids and in one week you are better just as the doctor promised.

People have followed me from four or five companies, and they still do what they shouldn't be doing. They still struggle with the same self-limiting beliefs they had with the company before and the previous company. It's baffling to me why they aren't doing what they know and need to do to be successful, the same things I have taught in the previous companies and am still teaching today

FIND YOUR POP

You must be excited about something and want it bad enough. Once your belief level gets to a place where you know that you can have success, and you know the results that other people have obtained, that's where suddenly the lights go on like crazy. A POP to me is a definition of a clarified point in my life; a point of passion where I know that I can do it. My mentor said to me, and I want to tell you, "you don't need a lot of reasons why something won't work for you. You only need one."

When you get that significant emotional event that POP, that place of passion, where you know that you can do this without a doubt; it comes very quickly. It all starts, believe it or not, by you just being aware that if others can do it, you can do it. Suddenly, it becomes comfortable.

Do you need to do it for somebody else and not yourself? Find the people you love the most who are closest to you. It could be a charity, a church, or a close friend. Say to them, "What can I do for you?" We will do more for them than for ourselves. You have to put your life on the line a little bit. When you know the things you want, you will forget about your time wasters, which don't matter anymore.

What if your life depended on it where suddenly you or a loved one didn't feel well, visited the doctor, and the doctor said, "You are going to die?"

You ask him, "How long do I have?"

He informs you, "You have about a month or two unless you lose weight, quit smoking and...." I'm sure you would do what the doctor tells you.

IS YOUR LIFE WORTH LIVING?

A personal story is when my mother first found out she had cancer. As mom and I sat in front of the doctor, the doctor asked my mom something which rocked our world, "Before we figure out a plan for treatment and before we go through the radiation and chemotherapy, I need to ask you one question. I don't want you to answer right away. I need you to think about this."

My mom quietly said, "Okay."

Her doctor asked, "How bad do you want to live?" Mom and I cried as the doctor counseled, "If you want to live, you are going to have to want it bad. You are going to go through much to stay alive. At the beginning when you start the treatments, you are going to wish you were dead; but you have to fight to live."

I'm asking you to do something that is simple. All you must do is ask a simple question to a bunch of people or just one person who may need your help. You aren't fighting for your life like my mom was.

TAKE CHARGE OF YOUR LIFE- YOU CAN DO IT!

When you see that you aren't doing all you need to do to reach your goals, would you stop saying I don't have the tools; I wish I knew what to do; I wish I had more personal development; I'm not sure this company is a good fit for me...None of this is the issue. You can be happy and prosperous. You can be anything you want to be. You can learn to change your mind. You can change your thoughts. You can be a winner! It's easy! The choice is yours.

God loves you, I love you, and pray for your success daily!

<u>Questions for Reflection:</u>

*Do you know what you truly want in life?

*Do you take shortcuts in reaching your goals?

*What is an example in your life where you want something, but you aren't doing the things it takes to make it happen?

*What is a POP you've had in your life

-CHAPTER TEN-

DESTROY YOUR LIMITING BELIEFS

"For the Spirit God gave us does not make us timid, but gives us power, love, and self-discipline."

2 Timothy 1:7

Do you feel stuck? Why are you not doing the things you know to do? Are your limiting beliefs holding you back? Everything you do has to do with a level of your belief. If you don't have faith, you aren't going to act on it.

One example is we all know people or have known people scared of dating. I don't know of one person in my entire life, as I grew up, who wasn't afraid at one point of asking someone out on a first date or going on one. It's paralyzing. For those of you who have been out on a date or many dates or those of you who have been on dates which ended in marriage, for those of you who not only got married but had a family, you got over your fear. The thing is you are never going to like and want to do it. I feel people struggle with having a *"why that makes you cry"*. You hear you need a purpose and a vision. You have all these things that are supposed to pull you through. Those are great, but as I previously mentioned, people need to know what they want first.

Successful people journal and unsuccessful, unhappy, and broke people don't. It's incredible to me! God rewards you for acting. It says in the Scripture if you have a lack of vision, you perish. It also said Moses wrote God's vision on tablets. If you aren't journaling every day, you should choose to begin and stop fighting what already works for others.

Just like gravity, the law of attraction, and success works. If you apply the laws of *Science of Getting Rich* the way successful people do, it's going to work for you. The rules include getting rid of your self-limiting beliefs. Most of the people I know when they became sick and tired of being sick and tired finally wrote down the things they were not willing to put up with anymore.

ENOUGH IS ENOUGH

Jim Rohn says it best, "You know you are pretty low when you lie to a Girl Scout." His story is the Girl Scout came to his door trying to sell him cookies. He told her he had already bought some. The reason Jim lied to this little Girl Scout is he didn't have any money to pay for cookies. He declared, "Enough is enough! I'm not going to live like this anymore!" His life changed when he lied to that girl scout. Do you have a story in your life similar to Jim Rohn and mine where you came to a crossroads where you declared, "Enough is enough?" I'm not going to live like this anymore!" An "enough is enough moment" is called a significant emotional event. Just this belief helps you go past your limiting beliefs.

Just like my story, it wasn't very long before Jim met Earl Schoaff because when the student is ready, the mentor appears. If you read my first book, you will have already heard my significant emotional event. My son asked me why wasn't I driving our car into the parking lot of our apartment building? I was ashamed to tell him that I was hiding it from the repo man. That was the day I didn't want to lie to my son anymore, and I didn't. I told him the truth, "I feel unworthy and worthless. All my decisions have gotten us here. I take 100% responsibility for where I am, and I promise I will never live like this again."

Where in your life do you need to take 100% personal responsibility for and say enough is enough?

THOUGHTS ARE THINGS

Are you consistently getting objections when talking to people? Not too many people like handling complaints, including me. We don't like people not showing up. We don't like people lying to us by telling us the things they think we want to hear. You accept someone else's opinions, thoughts, or beliefs over your own. You don't even know you are doing it, because this is not at a conscious level but on a subconscious level.

You will consistently attract individuals who come up with your limiting belief. An example of this would be someone saying, "I don't know anyone who has the money to get into this program."

I tell the person, "That's true because you haven't attracted anyone who has the money, because you believe no one has any money." The profession of an entrepreneur is going to be extremely difficult for you and you aren't going to get any results because of the words which come out of your mouth, "I can't afford it!" "I don't know anyone who can afford it!" Understand just because you have this limiting belief doesn't mean people aren't buying the product. Your limiting beliefs come from your thoughts and thoughts are things.

How do you destroy your limiting beliefs? Let me tell you a story from my life which may help you understand limiting beliefs. I had a guy who questioned and pressured me on my credentials. He didn't believe me. He asked, "Robert is it true when you first joined network marketing you made $10,000 in your first 45 days? It can't be a true story?"

I asked him, "Why would you think it wasn't true?"

He replied, "The majority of the people I know do not have this story. It took them a long time through personal development, getting rid of the limiting beliefs, and understanding the profession to have much success." When he questioned me, I asked myself why it worked quickly for me.

A TEMPORARY MINDSET

When I started in MLM, I didn't know much of anything about MLM or network marketing. I knew nothing about Amway or the other companies. I had never heard of them. The only thing I knew was my situation couldn't be much more desperate. When I first became involved in marketing, and an MLM company, I did it temporarily. I had a temporary mindset. I needed money and something I could do fast. I had no plans or intentions in any way, shape, or form of being a professional network marketer. I did not want to be on stage. I needed to make money as fast as I could.

More than likely, you've heard my story and know I only wanted to be an auto mechanic and a crew chief with race cars. My visions and goals didn't change, but I had a cast on my leg. I was collecting Workman's Comp where the Government paid me $900, a third of my regular pay. Money was tight.

Listen to my mindset at this time because I didn't want to do all these grandiose things other people wanted to do. I asked my mentor, "What are the steps I need to take to make money? I don't want to know anything else. I want a game plan on how I can make money and make it fast." What can I do to make money?

He replied, "Do you know my story?"

I answered, "Yes."

He mentored me and said, "You need to talk to people who have ears to hear and say as little as possible to as many people as you can. You will need to ask them if they know anyone who wants some extra money, edify, promote me, and let me do my job. If you put people in front of me, I'll get them to join."

I AM NOT HALF OF ANYBODY

"I will make you a challenge. Robert, I put 70 people in front of my mentor's presentation within the first 30 days and let's say you are half of me."

I interrupted him, "I'm not half of anybody. I accept your challenge."

I didn't have to handle many negative beliefs because I didn't want to know about the product, the comp plan, or the company story. The only information I wanted to know was what I needed to do to make money immediately. Nothing else mattered to me. My mentor told me if I found 2,000 people to watch his video, I would have success.

I remember as plain as day saying to him as I pointed my finger at him, "I'm going to get 2,000 people to watch this video, and when it doesn't work, I'm looking for you! I'm going to find you and get you."

He promised, "No, it will work."

Where did this limiting belief come from which hinted this might not work? It came from my past as I shared at the beginning of this book. My mentor proceeded to share with me his three-ring binder which had pictures of him and other successful people along with a colored copy of their checks. He showed me picture after picture of people who followed everything my mentor taught and had success.

SUCCESS STORIES

Do you struggle with limiting beliefs? The number one way to destroy your limiting beliefs is to study, memorize, and know other people's success stories. You have to know them like the back of your hand. You have to know them as you know your own story. Knowing success stories will help you handle any objections.

If someone says you are doing an illegal pyramid, you can tell a story about the businessman who got involved in your company and the success he had. You could say,

"Do you think this person with his credentials would get involved in something illegal?"

Someone else might question the product. You could tell that person about a lady in your company who has used that exact product and her results. If someone says, "I don't know anyone who has any money." You can say, "I understand, and I used to think the same way but here's what happened." You tell a story. Facts tell stories sell. When you have this whole list of stories, you can handle anything.

Be motivated and inspired to listen to other people's success stories repeatedly. I promise you regardless of your background, age, gender, or country you live in; you can be successful. Someone like you has already done what you are trying to do.

God loves you, I love you, and pray for your success daily!

Questions for Reflection:

*Is there a place in your life that you currently feel stuck?

*What limiting beliefs are keeping you stuck? What are you doing to get unstuck?

*Where in your life do you need to take 100% personal responsibility for and say "enough is enough"?

*What is a significant emotional event you have had in your life?

CHAPTER ELEVEN

DO YOU HAVE A CRAPPY STORY?

"I have told you these things so that in me you may have peace. In this world, you will have trouble. But take heart! I have overcome the world.

John 16:33

When I was growing up, I found out quickly I had a learning disability. People used to make fun of me, but I didn't have any idea what caused me to be different. I found out at the age of 28 I was dyslexic. I had a rough time reading, but I figured out ways of covering it up because I didn't want people to make fun of me.

Let's go back to limiting beliefs from the previous chapter. For anyone who has a disability or a limiting belief about who you are, put in a Google search for what is limiting you such as for me, successful people who are dyslexic. You will find when you do this; some millionaires and billionaires have the same disability or limiting factor you have in your life. How about successful people who dropped out of high school?

REPROGRAM YOUR THINKING

Another thing you need to understand about limiting beliefs is regardless of your age you have all this programming from your culture, environment, surroundings, and people. Did anyone ever speak into your life, "You won't amount to anything?" It happened to me over and over. Have people said negative things about you over the years? We think we can get rid of negativity, but we must reprogram our thinking. I want you to think of this one concept, "for things to change you must change". To achieve lasting powerful results and ultimately transform the quality of your life now and forever, you must adapt your ways of thinking, feeling, and acting. You must listen to new voices, ask new questions, put yourself in new states of thought and feeling, take further actions, get new results, and thereby gain a new perspective.

Some people may be uncomfortable and will make a conscious decision not to do any of it. It's hard to mentor someone who calls and tells you that they hate their life. All they want to do is share their past DVD over and over. They are very proficient at relating their crappy story. I know this sounds harsh, but I wish they would do me a huge favor and quit calling me. Now, listen to me carefully, that does not mean that I don't care. You will find that the more you get to know me, I care more about you than you will ever imagine. I care more about your success and your happiness than some of you who are reading this book right now. But you must stop making excuses because you have used those excuses and those distractions all the way up to this point. Some of you are not going to listen to me and will refuse to change. How can you get "gooder and gooder" if you won't let go of the past?

YOUNG BOBBY HOLLIS

My background starts out with trying to be the best kid I could be, but that would prove to be very difficult. I grew up in an alcoholic family. Life was tough as my parents fought all the time, and it always ended with my dad beating my mom. Every time my dad got drunk and beat up my mom, I also got hit.

My whole life all I can remember is when "this guy" got home, I needed to find a place to run and get away. I call him "this guy" because he wasn't a dad to me in any way, shape, or imagination. For him to feel he had a reason to beat me, he made demands I couldn't fulfill, nobody could.

An example of this was when he came home from work as a truck driver; he yelled, "You have an hour to mow the lawn."

The lawn he wanted me to mow wasn't even our lawn. It was the lot which sat next to ours, and we didn't even own it. It was impossible for me to mow this lot in one hour and "this guy" knew it. The kids in the neighborhood knew what was going on. When they heard me attempting to start the lawn mower, they quickly grabbed their lawn mowers and came over and tried to help me get the lot mowed in my one-hour time limit. They knew if I didn't make it happen, I would get beat. The sad thing is even with the neighbor kid's help, I never once pulled it off, so "this guy" beat me over and over again.

One of the many times "this guy" beat my mom, she ended up in the hospital. The state officials decided this was enough, and they locked "this guy" up. The last time I saw him, he talked to me through a little window, and told me, "I promise this will never happen to you again," which was the first promise he kept. When I was thirteen he disappeared, and he never beat me again, nor did I ever see him again.

DON'T GET CLOSE TO ME

As a thirteen-year-old, "this guy" was gone, so I started to believe everything was going to be okay and mom and my brothers could start a new life without fear. Unfortunately, this was not going to be the case. A couple of months after the police arrested "this guy," the court also arrested my mom for not protecting my brothers and me. They waited until she healed from the beating and then took her to jail. The social worker separated my two little brothers and me from my mom and placed us in separate foster homes. I jumped from foster home to foster home. I felt no one wanted me. The only thing I had registering in my mind is I sure don't want you to get close to me, because as soon as you do, you are going to leave me. Everyone always abandons me. Can you even imagine having to feel this way?

A COSTLY DECISION

People make choices, and not all these are good ones. Our decisions we make in life cause our uniqueness. Have you made bad choices in your life? At 17 years old, I made some awful ones. This could have ruined me for the rest of my life. Even though I made terrible decisions as a child, I eventually made good ones in my adult life. Listen to me; I don't want you to feel sorry for me. My crappy story turned out to be a blessing, made me who I am today, and most importantly my physical, emotional, and sexual abuse doesn't define me.

I went from high school to high school. In my senior year, I ended up back in the city where I grew up. I aimed to impress everyone. I needed to fit in and for people to like me. My Birthday was in February, so I concocted a plan so people would admire me, I had a great idea to throw a giant party, but it wasn't great at all. My plan: break into a warehouse, steal beer kegs, and host the most significant beer party anyone had ever seen. Sounds simple right?

I took some friends with me, and we broke into the warehouse. There weren't any kegs of beer there, but fortunately or unfortunately for us, there were semi-trucks parked in the warehouse with keys in the ignition. We opened the back of one of the trucks and couldn't believe our eyes. Cases of beer filled the inside of the semi from the bottom to the top. We knew it would be impossible for us to move this pallet of beer without someone catching us, but where there's a will, there's a way.

My genius, seventeen-year-old mind thought of a plan, which again I thought would be great. My friends would open the massive garage door, I would jump into the semi, back it up, and we would unload the semi at a couple of farms across the state line. We planned to store it there for a few weeks and then I would throw a huge Birthday party in February. That part of the plan turned out perfect. How could I honestly think this plan could work? I would have to say I wasn't thinking clearly and didn't realize there could be consequences for my actions.

A few weeks later, we had a giant party which ended up being big news and eventually touted in the Williston Herald as "Williston's Biggest Beer Bust"! Time went by after the party, and everything was quiet, so I thought I wasn't going to get in trouble. Little did I know "trouble" was right around the corner. I received a call from my friend, and he mentioned, "A leer jet just landed at our small airport. Eight guys got out of the jet wearing black jackets that had ATF on the back." (Alcohol Tobacco and Firearms) Trouble showed up!

CONSEQUENCES FOR MY ACTIONS

My problems were no longer in the authority of the little police department of Williston, N.D. The next thing I knew they arrested me, and charged me with 6 Class C felonies, each being punishable by five years and $100,000 fine. The Federal Government didn't care that I was a minor, they prosecuted me as an adult.

The judge told me since I'd never been in trouble before... let's digress a minute. No one ever caught me before. As a teenager, I didn't have money. I had this little thought in my mind that everyone had insurance so when I took their stuff, they could get it back, not from me, but the insurance company. Bad philosophy!

I did a plea agreement and got it down to one class C felony. They told me I would get a slap on the hand because it was my first offense. I had a court-appointed attorney, and everything seemed okay.

Two days before my graduation, the principal of the high school walked up to me and whispered, "Bobby, you've been a good influence on the people here. I'll make sure you graduate." I suddenly became confused. I went to my home study room, two sheriffs came in, arrested me in front of all the kids, and took me in for sentencing. I stood in front of the judge, and the judge reminded me, "According to this plea agreement, you promised you would cooperate with the courts."

"Yes, your honor I did."

"Who else helped you?"

"Helped me with what?"

"You didn't move 700 cases of beer yourself."

"Yes, I did your honor."

"I'll give you one more chance, who helped you?

My friends who helped me sat quietly in the courtroom and held their breath.

I repeated, "Your honor I did it myself."

The judge then counseled, "Is there any reason why we can't pass sentencing now?"

Everyone told him, "No."

"I sentence you to five years in the Federal Penitentiary, two to serve and three suspended. Take him away."

That was when my time in the federal penitentiary started. Do you think of me any differently? I tell you my story because as bad as this was, I made a choice not to let it define me. I don't share it for you to feel sorry for me. I was seventeen when this happened, and I am sorry for everything I did. Do you have anything in your past which is your crappy story?

I started meeting people who had lifetime prison sentences, and some had double and triple life sentences. I found out that my problems were not as severe as some of the inmates. You can always find people whose lives are way, worse than yours.

LEARN FROM YOUR MISTAKES

Six months later I went in front of the parole board. The lady asked, "Who would sentence a seventeen-year-old kid to two years in the federal penitentiary for his first offense? I told her the judge's name. She inquired, "Do you think you deserve your sentence?"

"I did wrong and yes I deserve it.

"If you weren't here, where would you be?"

"I enrolled in a North Dakota State School of Science and planned to be an engineer. It's just going to have to be two years later."

Even though the Federal Government doesn't usually give anyone cuts on their sentences, they gave me a year off my sentence. I spent 368 days thinking about who I wanted to be when I got out of prison. Fortunately, my story had a great outcome. Have you ever had a lot of time to sit and think about yourself?

After telling you my story, you can see that I could put my crappy story up against anyone else. I'd rather forget about my crappy story, and my goal is to get you not to

110

talk about your old DVD anymore. Now, I know this may be hard for you, but I want you to ask yourself what the payoff is? Do you get a payoff by telling your story? Do you believe that people pay more attention to you and feel sorry for you when you share your negative story? Decide to stop re-telling your negative story today.

My goal was to stop self-defeating myself, stop thinking about negative things, stop being a victim, and stop blaming situations, people, and anything else. I took personal responsibility for my life and said, "I messed up, and now I am going to work on getting "gooder and gooder. I began to follow documented mentors. I didn't have to do better all at once. I just had to get 1% better every day, so that I could be over 300% better in a year.

My negative past doesn't define me. What distinguishes me is the story I've created and am still building. I'd like to tell you about the number of people I've helped and will be assisting in the future, and testimonial after testimonial of people with changed lives who I have mentored. Instead of my crappy story, I'd like to tell you the story of how God has blessed my life in tremendous ways. What is the story you want to share?

In every crappy story, there is a potential gift, a seed of greater good, and a life lesson. The damage has been done. You can't reverse what happened, but you can move forward and choose to not let the adversity define you. Ask yourself, "What is the lesson I can learn through this trial in my life?" Crisis doesn't create character, it reveals it. You can move forward as a better, stronger person with a larger destiny for your life.

You are the best person you can be. You are not here by accident. You can do more, be more, and have more. You need to do the things which make you believe in your dreams. You must get past the thoughts of I don't feel like it, to I want to help more people. I can help you change your mindset.

FAITH IT UNTIL YOU MAKE IT

If you haven't put your own "I am statements" together, you need to do this right away. Write them down and take it one step further, look into a mirror, and say your I am statements as you look into your eyes. I am powerful! I am competent! I am capable! I'm a great friend! I am an awesome father or mother! I am an awesome leader! Affirmations are one thing but saying these statements with emotion and feeling is different. If you want to see my "I am statements", go to the end of this book. If saying your "I am statements" makes you super uncomfortable, know you are never going to feel like being successful. The successful people discovered they didn't feel right about doing whatever it took, but they did it anyway. They did it because they needed to change their current lifestyle.

According to Jim Rohn, success is 80% how you feel, how you think, and your intentions. When you learn to think differently, stop getting those limiting beliefs in your head, incredible things will happen.

My mentor told me if self-confidence issues, self-worth issues, and not feeling deserving of being successful and happy haunted me from my past, I needed to read *The God Memorandum* by Og Mandino. I bought the book right away and read the entire book in one sitting. I didn't let my dyslexia be an excuse for not doing all I needed to do. I wrote out *The God Memorandum*, and I read it every day. Type it out and have it on your computer screen to read every day aloud with emotion and feeling. It will get rid of old programming and put in the new programming.

Have you heard the quote "Fake it until you make it?" I like "faith it until you make it." Faith is speaking things that are not, as they are. I am going to be successful! I am a successful entrepreneur! I am an excellent speaker! I'm great at piquing interest! I'm fantastic at getting people excited enough to view the information! I'm good at doing a game plan! I'm good at inviting! Don't forget; I'm also a great looking guy! LOL

Are you working with the right people? You need to work with people who don't throw you in and tell you what to do. They need to be a mentor and friend to you, help you raise your standards and expectations, help you figure out your dreams and goals, and teach you how to make them happen.

God loves you, I love you, and pray for your success daily!

Questions for Reflection:

*If you have a crappy story, how often do you tell it?

*What is the payoff for sharing your crappy story?

*Have you put your "I am" statements together?

*Are you working with the right people?

-CHAPTER TWELVE-

UNCOMMON SENSE

"Blessed are those who find wisdom, those who gain
understanding."

Proverbs 3:13

I used to feel I needed to have common sense. I thought this was a good thing to have but have realized this isn't true. We all need to have the opposite of common sense, uncommon sense.

If you are common wouldn't you be like the other 99% of the people in the world who are clueless? Don't you hear all the time what do you have in common with other people? You want to be uncommon, not common, or ordinary. Has anyone ever asked you why you can't be normal, or have you said this to anyone? Find out why you are unique. If you don't know why you are special, you need to ask the people around you what they feel makes you unique. My whole goal is to help you find your uniqueness, your voice, and your inner story, which can inspire and motivate others to follow you.

You are special and unique. You have the ability, just as I, to inspire other people to greatness and dream again.

How many people do you know who need to believe they are great? Why would you want to be like everyone else? Why do you want to be normal? Why do you want to be common? When anyone asks you if you have common sense, your answer should be, "No, I don't have common sense! I have uncommon sense."

I took the time, and people mentored me who had a lifestyle where they gave more money to charity in a month than most people do in their lifetime. I want to travel the world, inspire people, help people make a difference when they leave this planet, and make people happy. I can show you the key to having an uncommon sense. Find out what everyone else is doing, do the exact opposite, and be unique and special.

FIND HIDDEN TREASURE

People who have uncommon sense are far more inspired by their dreams. They believe in hidden treasure and treasure maps. If you don't believe in treasure, don't think you will ever find it, and don't feel you deserve it, you already are in trouble. People find hidden treasure all the time. I love watching documentaries of people who find sunken ships full of riches. I can help you find your hidden treasure.

My mentor gave me a map. He promised, "Robert if you follow this map, you will find treasure."

Are you saying right now, "No, you didn't get a map. There's no treasure. Your mentor wouldn't give it to you."

That's a standard way of thinking. I had these same thoughts and many questions. My mentor pointed out, "I can show you how to find the treasure, and you will never have to worry about money again."

I had two questions for him: "What did you do before this, and how long have you been doing this?"

He told me he installed car stereos. Bummer, I wanted him to say he had been a rocket scientist or a brain surgeon. I looked for an excuse why I couldn't do it. In my mind I thought, if someone who installed car stereos could find the treasure, I knew I could locate it. The answer to my second question, he had only been with the company for three months. He showed me pictures after pictures of people with him holding their checks. Now, I saw not only that he had found the treasure, but now he had others who also had uncommon sense and found it.

I honestly never thought I could make or ever would make the amount of money my mentor did, but I needed to create something new and unique immediately in my life. I needed to develop the uncommon sense to make it happen. I was losing everything and didn't have any money. When I saw documentation, which showed my mentor made $62,000 a month, I knew my next move. I thought if I could make $4,000 a month, I would be able to pay my bills on time and slowly pull myself out of debt. I wasn't looking to earn $62,000. My common sense couldn't even come close to thinking this big.

Here is the next part I want you to understand. It blows my mind with the documented success I have had, and people won't follow my directions. I hand them the map, they won't even look at it, question if it is real, and wonder if the plan was followed the way I laid it out that they'd get the same treasure I received. Bottom line, they question themselves and doubt why I would give them the map. They think that God is a discerner of people and only Robert Hollis deserves to find the treasure. These thoughts are far from the truth! It is out there for anyone, including you, but you must follow the map.

THERE'S MORE THAN ENOUGH

Don't think I don't understand about a scarcity mentality and having common sense. I know it well because I used to be there. I found myself broke, selfish, worried, and self-centered. What set me apart from others, is I took the map, followed it without changing it, and discovered the treasure. Let me share a secret, I've seen the wealth, and more than enough is waiting for you, me, and everyone you and I know.

I'm handing you the plan and sharing the path you need to follow. What are you going to do with it? Are you scared to go where the map leads you, and make every excuse not to go on the journey? Will the past DVDs of your childhood prevent you from following the plan? Realize, you will meet people on the way who may not be interested in going with you. Don't allow people who aren't interested in following the map talk you out of following it. Don't let distractions and limiting beliefs keep you from pursuing it. I had many of the same distractions, so I know exactly how to get you from step one to step done in your journey. I can and will help you get rid of your limiting beliefs and begin believing in yourself. Take a leap of faith, follow the route, and find the treasure.

HELP PEOPLE FIND THEIR TREASURE

Listen to me! You must believe the treasure is there and you can share the map with people even before you find the treasure. The individual, who helps the most people, won't have to worry about their own needs at all. Do you think you need to reach it before giving others the map? What if it's about you getting other people there even if you still have limiting beliefs, don't love yourself, are lazy, and make excuses? What if the only thing you do is point people to me, and I give them the map? Imagine all of them coming back and giving you a piece of the treasure because you pointed them in the right direction and changed their lives.

What a concept! You must believe that I have already found the treasure and have helped many others locate it. Bottom line is you must realize your treasure is close, and if you carefully follow the map, you will see it. You need to have uncommon sense.

God loves you, I love you, and pray for your success daily!

Questions for Reflection:

*Do you have common sense or uncommon sense?

*Why do you feel you are special and unique?

*Is there anywhere in your life you have a scarcity mentality?

*Do you believe your treasure is close and you will find it?

-CHAPTER THIRTEEN-

THANK-YOU JIM ROHN

"Sow your seed in the morning and at evening let your hands not be idle, for you do not know which will succeed, whether this or that, or whether both will do equally well.

Ecclesiastes 11:6

When I say thank-you to Jim Rohn, it's emotional to me. The mentors who help us are fantastic! Mentors love assisting people every day to keep them from suffering. Seek out the counsel of mentors who are achievers. Become accountable to someone whose past performance earns your respect.

Jim interrupted the story I believed about myself. He empowered me to become as Mother Teresa would say, "A pencil in the hand of God writing a new chapter in his life." When Jim spoke, I saw the possibilities of not having to continue living the life I had been living. He taught me that my history didn't have to become my future. He showed me greatness, which nobody in my past had shared with me.

CONTENT PER MINUTE

The number one thing you need to do is find a mentor who not only has documentation of being successful but also, has helped other people become successful. I will never forget meeting my mentor, Jim Rohn when I was twenty-nine years old. I was also honored to work with him. The way I rate mentors, personal development, business philosophers, and wisdom is by content per minute. The world right now is drowning in information, but it lacks in wisdom. When I met Jim Rohn, he was a business philosopher. When I sat and listened to him, I had a tough time taking notes. The number of pearls of wisdom he dropped whenever he uttered anything was incredible! He would say, "Profits are better than wages." I quickly tried to jot that down, so I remembered it, but before I even got the word profits written, he said, "If you can't afford it, you can't afford not to." Everything he said was worthy of writing down.

Have you listened to or read anything Jim Rohn created? We live in this beautiful internet world where you can go to YouTube and search for Jim Rohn and watch him share his wisdom. I've always wondered how many times Jim had to write out what he wanted to say to have that many pearls of wisdom come out of his mouth every time he spoke. I wish I would have asked him.

In his seminars, he would ask the crowd, "How many people here are broke?" People raised their hands. He would then say, "Wow! Don't you feel sorry for yourself?" The people would agree with him. He would say something which makes me laugh every time, "At least you aren't ugly!" He then said, "For people who are broke and ugly there's always something which could be worse, at least you aren't sick." Everyone would laugh, and he would say, "You are poor, ugly, and sick, well at least you aren't stupid!" People have shared Jim Rohn's pearls of wisdom throughout the years.

GOD BROKE THE MOLD

I met Jim Rohn at a small event. He impressed me because it didn't matter the size of the crowd he spoke to, he didn't hold back and gave his best. I bought everything Jim Rohn created for the public and has ever sold. I wore them out because I couldn't get enough.

Jim Rohn impacted hundreds of millions of people and still affects people now that he's gone. Greats like Tony Robbins, Les Brown, Bob Proctor, Zig Ziglar, Brian Tracy, and Steven Covey showed up for Jim Rohn's tribute when he left this world. Each of these leaders took their turn and spoke on stage as they shared their love and admiration for Jim Rohn. We all did our best to immolate him and try to be as good as him, but I feel God broke the mold with him. I will never forget Les Brown when he walked on stage at Jim Rohn's tribute. He told the crowd about his first big seminar where Jim sat in the audience. After Les had finished the first fifteen minutes of his training, he stopped and looked over at Jim, "Jim why are you taking notes?"

Jim became puzzled, "What are you talking about?"

Les asked again, "Jim, why are you taking notes?"

Jim pointed out, "Well this is awesome information! It's some of the best information I have ever heard!"

Les Brown declared, "It's yours, Jim!"

Jim didn't miss a beat and replied, "It's still good stuff!"

I am honored and blessed that I worked directly with Jim Rohn. I believe 1000% my results show that.

DOCUMENTATION BEATS CONVERSATION

I learned from a few of my mentors, Jim Rohn, Bill Gouldd, and Roger Penske that documentation beats conversation. These people would flat out document your brains out! They got your attention immediately because they showed their success.

Here is the next level. Jim Rohn said, "If you want to be successful beyond your wildest dreams, you have to make sure when people write their testimonial or say it in audio or video, you want to make sure your name shows up in it." The main thing I have prided myself in is I have currently helped over 50 people make over a million dollars. I moved into an apartment where I trained identical twins, Mike, and Tony Coupisz. Today they own a company where they do over 800 million dollars. They are growing at over 100 million dollars a year. Most importantly, you need to find a mentor documented in helping others.

THE HUMBLEST MENTOR

I hope Jim Rohn had an idea of how much he meant to me and still does. He not only set the bar on content per minute, but he is also the one I look up to as being the humblest.

My mentor, Bill Gouldd, whom I also looked up to, had a different personality than me. He was an A-type personality and was rough. If I called him and asked for a couple of minutes of his time, he would have to check my volume printout before he would talk to me. Bill wouldn't give me a minute of his time if I weren't listening to his audios, watching the videos, applying what he taught, and getting results from them. I found out red personalities, driven, hardcore closers, and recruiters did not fit my style. I knew I needed to find someone with my style because I'm not money motivated. When I met Jim Rohn, I could see his personality exemplified being nice, sincere, soft-spoken, and humble. I connected with him on a deep level. Jim said, "People don't care how much you know until they know how much you care." He exemplified this!

I try my best to immolate the Jim Rohn style because I want people to know I care. I know the more I give, the more I get. If you're going to be successful, you must find a mentor who cares. You need to find a documented mentor and people who are willing to give credit to this mentor.

THE ULTIMATE GOAL

Jim Rohn gave me the opportunity to ask him a question which impacted me. I asked him, "What is the ultimate goal?"

He answered, "Robert, if you work super hard on you, one day you will walk into a room and will hear people say, there he is! There's the guy right there! You will walk through hotels and airports and at conventions and hear people yell, "There's Robert Hollis!"

Many times, I've been in hotels and airports where people have stopped me and said with tears in their eyes, "Robert your videos impacted me deeply and had changed and altered my life! I know I can do this and make it work! Thank-You!" Even though I know I'm not a smidgeon of Jim Rohn, I know I'll work my heart out for the rest of my life building a legacy.

One day when I pass, I pray and believe my maker, my God, will be standing there and asking me, "Robert why should I let you into Heaven?" Even though my dream may not be scriptural, I want hundreds of thousands of people who I've made a difference in their lives, saying, "Let him in! Let that guy in! He has devoted his life to helping people and making a difference!" I love helping people. I want my Maker to look at me and say, "Well done my good and faithful servant!" Thank-you, Jim Rohn, for impacting my life in more ways than I can even say!

God loves you, I love you, and pray for your success daily!

<u>Questions for Reflection:</u>

*Who do you consider to be your mentor or mentors?

*Is your mentor proven and documented? Have you seen his or her documentation?

*Is your mentor documented with helping others be successful?

*What legacy do you wish to leave?

-CHAPTER FOURTEEN-

THE WINNER IN YOU!

"Let us not become weary in doing good, for at the proper
time we will reap a harvest if we do not give up."

Galatians 6:9

Are you playing with the life you have? Start existing
and living, because you are a winner and can be
successful and happy. Do you realize how many people
don't work on their personal development? They never ask
for help or know it even exists. They are too busy being
busy. For you taking the time to read this book, it already
puts you in a high percentage. I would say, based on all I
know, you are easily in the top 10% of the people on the
planet because you took the time to better yourself.
Congratulations to you! I'm super proud of you!

DEFENDING YOUR LIFE

Let me share with you for a fact why I know and
believe you are a winner. First, I want you to imagine for
a minute a movie of your entire life is playing. It includes
the good times, tough times, and everything else. What if
you had to defend certain things in your life before moving
on to the next life? What if you had to defend your life as

the movie "Defending Your Life" with Meryl Streep? Imagine sitting in front of a Prosecutor and a Defense Attorney. The Defense Attorney pulls things up as you watch the movie of your life. He takes you clear back to when you attended school. For whatever reason you weren't paying attention in class, you didn't study enough, and didn't do all you felt you needed to do to pass the critical test. The night before the test, you focused, read the things you should have read already, and you studied hard. Because of your diligence, you passed the test. You felt as if you won.

As you continue watching your life movie, you realized school was tough for you. You also weren't the most popular kid in the class. You watch your life movie and say, "Another win, I made it through school!" You see people in your film whom you had made a difference in their lives. As they speak, you didn't realize how big a difference you made. You see yourself helping a sad and depressed friend feel better by spending time with her and telling her positive, happy stories. It changed her state just because you cared about her. Here's another win! You saw yourself becoming a good athlete. Even though people didn't think you could do it, you took the time to practice, you made the winning basket, and as you watched, you remembered that feeling all over again. Again, you won!

As you watch your movie, you see times you felt on top of the world, and everything worked out. It's hard to remember the good and unique times when you are walking through the challenging times. You watch the special times in your life, for instance when you got married. Getting married to my love, Teri, became one of my giant wins and one of the most significant victories of my life.

As you watch your movie, you see your children as they grow up and consider their lives a huge win. My boys, daughters-in-law, and grandchildren are a huge win! A win for you could be you found a job you love with the ability to pay your bills every month. As you watch your movie in your mind what are your wins and victories? Some people's fear, anxiety, worry, self-limiting beliefs, and stinking thinking are not helping them to become successful. Don't let others define success for you. Only you can identify and create it.

The reason I'm having you watch your movie is because I want you to understand you have had times in your life where circumstances seemed tremendous and worthy of celebrating. You have it within you to be a winner again and consistently win where you go from victory to victory. You watch your movie and see something which didn't go as you wished it did. You always figured a way to turn these past negative scenes around and still got through them, so that was a win. You read my crappy story, but I've covered up that story by the awesome memories I have.

I'm not asking you to do something you can't do. When you think of being an entrepreneur you connect with people and build relationships; you can do that. You create a connection where the person knows, likes, and trusts you; you can do that. You care enough where the person wants to buy your product and service, wants to support you, and wants to be in business with you; you can also do that.

Some people don't view getting a check as a victory. I did because I was coin-operated where I worked for someone else's dreams. I was only an employee, but when I did everything my mentor told me to do and received my first check as an independent contractor in the company I was with, it was like "Bingo!" I knew there was a great deal I needed to learn, and I knew beyond a doubt, I could learn it.

First, I want you to think about what I am asking you to do. I am asking you to use your mouth. I have helped people who couldn't talk. I've helped people who couldn't hear or see. I've supported people with all kinds of disabilities, including a person with quadriplegia. You can figure out ways to find out what anyone wants and show them how to do it. All you must do is learn to connect with people you don't know. That's the key! Keep giving and trust if you continue to build a brick at a time, one day you will have a wall.

You must believe if other people have done it, you can do it too. I know you can win this game. Why? It's because I know my story.

IT STARTS WITH AN IDEA

One of my favorite shows to watch is Shark Tank. If you haven't watched episodes of the Shark Tank, I feel you should. I almost think it should be mandatory for anyone I mentor to watch it. One of the things you must realize on Shark Tank is people show up on the show with only an idea. Most of the time they have no money, no product, and no patents. They tell their story. My wife, Teri, and I watched an episode where an entrepreneur made little lenses and placed them on cameras. He reinvented this idea and put them on drones. The Sharks asked him how long he had been doing this.

"Dude, I went to Santa Barbara and used to be on the California ski team." All the Sharks laughed at him because he talked like a surfer dude. He continued, "Like Dude man I make these accessories, battery operated selfie stick. Suddenly I took pictures, and the professional pictures looked better than mine. I found out they used filters. I took the filters and made them for drones."

The Sharks weren't impressed at all and asked," Is there a market for this?"

Finally, Mr. Wonderful couldn't take it anymore and asked him, "How long have you been in business?"

"I've been in business for 11 years."

One of the Sharks asked him, "What have you done for sales?"

"Listen to this dude, my first year I did $8000 in sales."

They all laughed hard at him. They proceeded, "What did you do last year?"

The guy couldn't wait to tell them, "I made 3.2 million dollars."

The Sharks asked him, "How much money did you borrow?"

"I used $2000 from my student loan, and that's the only money I've ever borrowed."

Now all the Sharks loved him, and they ended up fighting for him because the company was debt free, did 3.2 million dollars last year and will do 5 million this year.

My point to this story is this entrepreneur built a 3.2-million-dollar business with student loan money. He did it with an idea and demanding work. I can tell you story after story of people like me who became successful by merely being able to use their mouth, get excited, promote, and edify someone other than them.

You must be able to tell a story and invite somebody to a video or a system. Wow! How difficult is that? You encourage people to do this all the time. How often do you ask someone to watch a funny, exciting, or inspirational video you like? Maybe you tell someone about a sermon online or a favorite song. You say check it out because it inspired you.

Get enthusiastic about talking, sharing, inviting, promoting, and edifying. Say aloud, "I am a winner! I will succeed! I will get gooder and gooder every day in every way!" What you are asking a person to do is simple. Why people complicate things around the world is beyond me but guess what? I do it too.

YES, I'M HUMAN!

An example of this comes around tax time. I'm the kind of guy who has accountants, tax people, lawyers, and bookkeepers. Every year they do everything for me.

They put my portfolio together and before tax time get in touch with me and say, "Robert we have a question about this transaction, where did this money go and who is this person and this person?"

As soon as I get the paperwork and open it, I see thirty or forty transactions marked. I get a little anxious and worked up and say, "Oh No! I have to look online and find all these transactions, and I have to look at my statements and find receipts." I think it's complicated and going to take a long time to do, so I procrastinate and put it off until the final minute. Yes, I'm human.

Messages come that there will be penalties and interest charged if I don't get the information to my tax people. I open it, and it takes me 5-10 minutes to find the necessary information. Why didn't I open it right away and knock it out in 5-10 minutes? Yes, I'm human. Is there anything in your life you do the same thing with where you procrastinate until the last minute?

GETTING YOUR MOJO BACK

How can you get your mojo back? The important thing is you don't need anything. Everything you need to be a winner is already inside you. You are great! It's the people who come up with their self-limiting beliefs who think they need something outside themselves. Do you find yourself saying, "I need this and this and this?" If you let the words "I need" come out of your mouth, you are in trouble.

What can you personally do daily to stay in the winner mentality? Let me share with you what I do, and it might help you to design a plan for your life. I start with reading my "I Am statements". I also listen to the book my mentor told me to read, *Science of Getting Rich* I've heard it so many times; I have it memorized. I watch YouTube videos of every kind of success story you can imagine. I find stories of people who declared they couldn't do something, and they did it anyway and became successful. These people touched many people and ended up giving a tremendous amount of money to charity.

I spend time listening to stuff which amps me up. Do you have a favorite movie you like to watch or an inspirational and motivational song you love? I have two favorite songs. One of them is "Say Amen," and the other is by Rascal Flatts called "My Wish for You." Both these songs immediately amp me up and get me into a fantastic state.

I take control of my state. You have the power over your state, but you must get your mind in the right place. When you stop making excuses, know what you want, and believe in yourself, you will have control. You will figure out the things you need to do and do them as much as you can every day. If you want to be good at anything, you need to practice. If you want to be a good singer, it takes practice. If you want to be above average at anything, you must practice.

I GIVE YOU PERMISSION

You are a winner! I'm proud of you and give you permission to be happy, successful, replace your income, give to charity, and travel the world. I give you right now permission to love yourself and accomplish anything you want to do. If no one has ever given you permission to do great things in your life and be a winner, I just did. If you haven't done it yet, it doesn't mean it's not going to happen. Look at everything you have done in your past and throw it away and start doing it right now. Hang around people who believe you can. My mentor believed in me and gave me the same permission, so I'm returning the favor.

You already know from the movie of your life you watched you've been a winner in the past, and you can get your mojo back. You need to do the things daily to get yourself in a positive, happy, enthusiastic, state of mind. You must know what you want and learn to want it bad. Go out there, make a difference, and lead by example. Show the world life is more than surviving and existing.

God loves you, I love you, and pray for your success daily!

Questions for Reflection:

*What do you view in your life as a victory?

*What do you need to do to have a winner mentality?

*What is the motivation you use to amp yourself up?

*When you watch the movie of your past, what comes up? Is it mostly sad, regret and defeating or happy and motivating?

CHAPTER FIFTEEN

HALL OF FAME

"Commit to the Lord whatever you do, and he will establish your plans."

Proverbs 16:3

Have you heard of the Hall of Fame? How about the Rock n Roll Hall of Fame, Baseball Hall of Fame, Basketball Hall of Fame, Football Hall of Fame, and many others? What Hall of Fame is someone going to induct you into? How about the Spouse Hall of Fame, the Friend Hall of Fame, or the Parent Hall of Fame? Shouldn't you be thinking about that?

We are only here for a brief period. When you leave this planet what are you going to be known for? Don't you think that is important? Some people, unfortunately, will be in the Survival Hall of Fame of people who barely made it and just survived. How about the not much in debt Hall of Fame? How about give as little to charity and other people Hall of Fame? Come on!

WHAT WILL YOU BE KNOWN FOR?

I always had a goal of one day getting on stage for my company. I figured if I made a big enough difference in the company, the owner might ask me to come on stage. I knew it would all start on a small scale like the stage of a local Saturday training or a regional. If I stayed focused and helped more people, I knew I could get on stage at a national event and an International event. I can remember seeing the people on stage and imagining being up there myself. I knew I needed to follow all they did to get on the stage.

Much faith, skill, belief, preparation, and action helped me get there. After I reached those goals, I set other goals. What if I could be in the top 10 of the company on stage? When I arrived at my goal, I thought wouldn't it be cool if I was one of the top five recognized on stage. I did that. My next goal was to become the top 3 in the company and my ultimate goal, the number one person in the company. I did that and held the position for a few years. What would be next?

I'm not saying any of this to brag. I'm telling you that there are things which are set up in this day and time that you should at least try to pull off before you go. Find the people who have pulled it off and follow them. God is not a discerner of persons; if they can do it and I did it, you can do it.

I said, "Okay, I've reached all those goals what is next?" I thought it would be cool if the company recognized me on a generic stage. I started out being on a panel, and suddenly I had the honor and privilege to be an anchor speaker for a crowd of 8,000 network marketing professionals at the Eric Worre Go Pro event. Every time I reached a goal, I needed to visualize and be passionate about doing something new in my life.

When you die, what are you going to be known for? What is everybody going to be talking about when you leave? Is it going to be a grand celebration as Jim Rohn says? When people tell their story either in written form, verbally, or in a video are they going to talk about you? Are they going to talk about you with admiration because you showed bravery as you reached out to them, and connected them with a mentor who helped them be able to visualize and get that POP (point of passion)?

My next big win was writing my first book, (*How Is That Working?*). I became a bestselling author with #1 on Amazon in a couple of categories. I mentioned Sean Hennigan in my first book and a previous chapter of this book. Sean was a guy I didn't get a chance to know well, but he dared to get past his fears and self-limiting beliefs by reaching out to me to help me which was critical to my success! Think about what you are going to be known for.

EJECT YOUR PAST DVD'S

Let's talk about you getting inspired, having hope, and dreaming again. You can make this the best year you've ever had. Are you talking about your past DVDs', good or bad? People brag about being a great athlete in high school. Every time you talk to them, they reminisce about the best times in their lives that have already happened. That is sad! It's good to have those good times, but you need to have those good times which take your breath away now. It's your time!

If you could talk to your younger self what advice would you give? If I could go back and talk to young Bobby, I would tell him to think bigger faster and stop doubting himself and his abilities. If I had done this, I would have accomplished much more than I had with not much more effort. I would have worked smarter instead of harder. Since I can't change anything in my past, I need to move to live in my present instead of the "what if" world.

You don't want to talk consistently about your lousy old DVD of last year. Was last year challenging for you? I must help you let go of the victim mentality because if you live in the past or you live each day talking about all the things that are wrong and the dreadful things that happened to you, it will be hard to be successful in the present. It's wild because we live in a world right now where people get to name all the stuff they are.

I get people that call me and say, "Listen I need your help. You wouldn't believe I need money tomorrow. I'm losing money on everything. I'm ADHD, I'm dyslexic, I have some disorder, and I, I, I, I,." They already have framed their entire life in a box. Someone else labeled them, and you know how difficult it is to help somebody that believes that they can't do anything? They can't be successful. They can't change their spots because someone else told them about the DVD in their head. If it was a good year, let's not replay that either. Let's eject your DVD and talk about what you are going to do in the future. What Hall of Fame do you want to be in? Figuring this out should be part of your thoughts and vision all the time. Here is the point I want to make. Stop saying it's too late. It's not too late. You are not a failure nor a loser. You are not too old. No! Quit labeling yourself!

SIMPLE KEY TO SUCCESS

The key to success is simple. You must fall in love with your vision and dream, find people who have pulled it off, and become disciplined and coachable. You must believe in your heart if God has allowed other people to pull it off, He's not keeping it from you. You are keeping it away from you. It's there right now in your grasp. Today faster than any time in history money is made. If you haven't grabbed onto the thought of your goals and what Hall of Fame you are going to be in, you should do it NOW. Plug into someone who believes in you and knows you can make it to your Hall of Fame. Hopefully, by reading this book, you are on the path to "getting gooder and gooder". I have the treasure map, and my deepest desire is to help you discover your treasure.

God loves you, I love you, and pray for your success daily!

Questions for Reflection:

*What Hall of Fame will you be known for?

*How can you make this your best year ever?

*Have you fallen in love with your visions and dreams?

*Are you disciplined and coachable?

CHAPTER SIXTEEN

NEVER SAY NEVER

"For I know the plans I have for you," declares the Lord, "plans to prosper you and not to harm you plans to give you hope and a future."

Jeremiah 29:11

"I'm done. I love network marketing, but I hate network marketing owners!" I previously in my career built up seven companies where I was the top income earner and top sponsor, and my team leaders made full-time incomes. All seven-company owners made stupid decisions which not only caused my income to decrease, but it destroyed my team leader's income and made me a liar. (Definition of insanity: "doing the same thing over and over and expecting a different result.") I have retired from network marketing. I choose to focus on my coaching, training and promoting my Robert Hollis brand. I vowed I would never join another company."

Until.... my wife, Teri, whom I dearly love, who has never complained and supported me throughout all these companies for thirty years, asks for my help. She had become an empty nester and wanted to make money to pursue her passion, animal shelters, and rescue animals. We have been blessed to build a substantial nest egg, but Teri didn't want to dig into it. We had spent much of our life barely making it, so it is tough to dig into our nest egg because we feel like failures, because we still can generate income. She had watched me make money in the network marketing space, so she decided to make her own money in network marketing. I told her to go for it, even though she knew how I felt about joining another company. She picked a few companies but didn't have any success. I watched her struggle, so I reviewed the companies and found out they were all old-school marketing, what I had previously left. Some of the companies even forbid her from doing online marketing.

MY CRITERIA TO PROMOTE A COMPANY

Teri finally came to me and said, "Robert, tell me what I need to do. You have had success in all those other companies, so teach me how to do it."

Teri and I had a husband and wife moment where I giggled at her, and she didn't appreciate it. Teri said, "Just tell me what to do without hype or BS."

"First you need to find a company in momentum. Then you need to find distributors in the company who follow the company system and have moved up the ranks, making money fast in weeks and even days. You need to find someone who will show you their documented checks and how many people have rank-advanced in their group. My definition of a good company is what the leaders say about the owners. Find a company that is marketing using today's technology.

Teri said, "Well then if you are such a smart-aleck, you go find that company."

Finding Teri's next company became a challenge for me. I hadn't even looked for a company since 2012, but I wasn't about to tell the love of my life no, so I decided to find Teri a company that met my qualifications. I did my due diligence and reached out to the top distributors, not the owners. My definition of a good company is what the leaders say about the owners. After my extensive research, I told Teri, "I've chosen the company you need to join."

Her next question rocked my world, "Why don't we do it together?"

I wasn't prepared for that because I had retired from network marketing. My goal was to find any excuse not to do it. I told Teri, "Let's reach out to the owners." I knew that would be the downfall of the company, because of my previous experience with owners. Immediately, the owners of the company we were looking at, got on a zoom call with us. In the back of my mind, I hoped the conversation would change our minds about joining the company. It was quite the opposite. Every answer from the owners made us more excited.

MOST IMPORTANT TOOL

It doesn't matter how good a product is, if there isn't a great system in place, I won't even look at it. The word system stands for: Save Yourself Time Energy & Money. When the owners started explaining their company's operation, it blew Teri and me away. Their system allows affiliates to give away something for free, which is a test drive, a tour, of the company. This fit right into my philosophy of being a go-giver. Another important aspect of a great system is a fear of loss where the company does the first follow-up for you. People don't duplicate, systems do.

Many people believed I couldn't re-do the massive success I had before in other companies, and they didn't think I could help people duplicate success in this company. I wanted to prove them wrong. Despite the rumors, we paid our way into the company with no deals. We wanted to start like everyone else so we could show we could have success beginning at zero. The rest is history.

TIMING BEATS EVERYTHING

In 5 months, duplicating precisely what I shared in this book, I helped Teri go from 5K to 10K, to 25K to 50K to 100K to 250K in volume on a company that pays out 85%. In the first 5 months, Teri with the help of her team had made over $100,000 and was #5 in the company. I've never seen a more lucrative pay plan and seen more people rank advance so quickly, which makes me most excited.

This company is at the perfect place at the perfect time and my opinion the product has rocked my world. Timing beats experience, wisdom, and hard work. It's all about timing and action.

In my experience, I have found that it is essential to keep my mind open like a parachute, and never say never to opportunities that are at the right time and place.

MY FINAL THOUGHTS

BE GRATEFUL!

For the past over thirty years, I am so grateful that I have owned my own time. I realized early on that time was my most valuable asset, and I could never get more of it, so I must value what I have. I had no boss tell me what to do, no supervisor to check in with, and no debt to keep me up at night. My life is nothing short of a dream. In fact, my reality now is better than my dreams used to be. Never could I have imagined all that life had to offer.

Today I'm also grateful for financial freedom which comes with its options. There is a saying, "There is a difference between making a living and making a life." I have a life and love it. What I am most proud of is that my success has affected others' success. What are you most grateful for in your life?

DON'T SETTLE

I plead with you not to settle. No matter what your life story is, no matter where you are, you can start now to change your future. Make this the first day of the rest of your life. None of us can go back and change our past, but we can all start today and make a new beginning. Keep dreaming and most importantly, keep working and aspiring to be, do, and have more. That is my prayer for you.

Take note of how far you have come, what you have accomplished in your life, and how much you have left to do. You can't afford to waste a year, a month, or even a day in the pursuit of your dreams. Don't dream your life away. Although it's important to imagine, don't get caught up in the quest of planning and dreaming without action.

CHANGE STARTS WITH YOU

Make positive changes in your personal, business, and spiritual life so you can make a difference in the world. It starts with you, but it doesn't start until you act. Choose to change! Expect success! Get "gooder and gooder" every day in every way.

For everyone who turns a disadvantage into an excuse, there is someone else who turns it into their trampoline to success and greatness. We don't have choices about what happens to us, but we always have options what we are going to do about it.

If you knew, beyond a shadow of a doubt, that you would be changed and impacted forever by the people, places, social media, and the environment around you, would you look at your life differently? If you knew that you were going to become like the people you hang around and take on their characteristics, would you consider changing the group of people you hang around? If you knew the negative information you exposed yourself to on a daily basis would affect your outlook, direction, and your personality, wouldn't you begin to view more positive information and not let people and technology back a garbage truck into your mind?

BE A GO-GIVER

As you go through your day, find special and unique ways to be a go-giver. It will show people how you feel, but more importantly, it will change the way you think about yourself. If you focus on reaching your goals by helping people achieve their goals and meeting the needs of others, you can't fail.

You and I have the opportunity every day to reach out to hundreds of people with an encouraging word, an act of kindness, or by merely taking a few minutes to listen to someone with your heart. You have the opportunity and responsibility to positively impact the lives of others, not only with products and services but by being an example. Reach out to someone and make a difference in their lives and yours.

Remember to follow the path of individuals who have already proven themselves to be successful. I want you to know from this day forward, I believe in you, your success, and your destiny. Make a positive move towards your success.

MOVE TOWARD YOUR GREATNESS

If you are not where you want to be along your road to success, you may want to examine not only how hard you are working, but what you are doing. Are you doing the things that you need to do to move you forward? Are you doing the things that successful leaders do?

Work on being known for one thing and doing it exceedingly well. Build your success from there. Life rewards us for doing one thing very well and then building on that success to have other achievements in the future. Move towards your greatness and move away from what makes you average and ordinary.

Trust that you don't know what you don't know. Make today the first day of the rest of your life. Believe that you are unique. Figure out what you want and believe you are free. Destroy your limiting beliefs and get rid of your past DVDs and crappy story.

Allow yourself to have an uncommon sense as you find the winner in you. Figure out what hall of fame you want to be inducted into and follow a documented mentor to help get you there. If no one has ever given you permission to get "gooder and gooder" and go from shackled to free, I give it to you now.

Each day is a gift from God, and we never know when our time may be up. Pursue your dreams and goals with all the energy, joy, and passion you possess. You have your desires for a reason. Each day you must progress toward your visions, so invest in your future today.

God loves you, I love you, and pray for your success daily!

ACKNOWLEDGMENTS

With Special Thanks:

Foremost, I want to thank God for the wisdom he has bestowed upon me, strength, peace of mind, and good health throughout my life. Thanks also to my prayer partners.

Teri, I am especially grateful for your love, prayers, and undying support throughout the years. You are my life!

Robert Hollis Jr, Matthew, Kyle, Amy, and Hannah. Thank you for encouraging me in all of my pursuits and inspiring me to follow my dreams. To my grandkids, I love you more than you will ever know.

Thank-you Laurie Monson for imparting your knowledge and expertise in co-authoring this book. Steve Monson thank-you for your expertise in creating the powerful book cover design. Matthew Hollis, thank-you for everything you do to make me look good.

To all the individuals I have had the opportunity to lead, mentors I've been trained by or influenced by as I watched their leadership from afar, Thank-you for being the inspiration and foundation for Shackled to Free! Getting Gooder & Gooder!

PRAISE:

"Robert is a real student of what success is all about. Robert, you are the man." Eric Worre

"Robert is an excellent network marketer and a genius mentor. He has crushed it in the network marketing industry. He has arguably created more millionaires than maybe anyone inside of network marketing. He is an absolute rock star, and we are so honored to work with Robert. Thanks, Robert for all you do!" Ray Higdon

"Robert Hollis is a guy who is a great friend and mentor. I take his word and suggestions often. This man has built multiple millionaires, but also has been consistent with his training, consistent with how he feels about the industry, and consistent about how he cares for people." Armand Puyolt

"I was struggling with marketing for years until I met Robert in 2000. At that time, he was the #1 producer in the company. He shared with me how to find the right people and everything changed quickly for me. Robert understands people and marketing." Paul Henderson

"When Robert coached me and taught me his formula, I earned millions. I started my own company in 2013 and life continues to get better every day. Robert is an amazing friend and mentor, thank you! Listen to Robert!" Joven Cabasag

Immediately I was drawn to Robert's message and his sincerity. I was blown away by how sincere, and down to earth, he was. I knew this was a mentor I wanted to follow. When I got back to South Africa, Robert became one of my biggest mentors. I can honestly say if I hadn't plugged into his teachings, I wouldn't have been where I am now. I am so thankful for what Robert taught me. Andrew Eaton

You changed my life, gave me direction, helped me replace my full-time income within my first 60 days while working with you. Learning from you while you believed in me until I could believe in myself is PRICELESS! Thank-you Robert for being my friend, mentor, and having a Heart of Gold! Meladee Ryba

"Robert is the man! Seeing him as a mentor to so many top earners in this industry, he isn't just a multi-millionaire, but he's helped 40-50 people become millionaires. That to me is what is so impressive. He's a mentor's mentor and a leader's leader. Robert, I appreciate you, brother." John Melton

"To know Robert is to love him. He is so genuine and is truly there to connect with you and help you. We love him and highly recommend him and everything he does. Thanks, Robert!" Nadya Melton

"Robert thank you for everything you've done for my family and me in our lives and being there for us and mentoring us. I just wanted to let everyone know what a huge-hearted, genuine person you are. You are a legend in this industry. You are an excellent friend, and we consider you family." Jun Lee

"My friend and mentor Robert Hollis helped me realize my gifts and talents and abilities I was downplaying and wasn't making the most of. I love that I can have someone who can take that personal time to invest in me and pour into me and my business so that I can turn around and be a blessing to others. You can't ask for more than that." Wanda Kay

"Robert goes way above and beyond. It's much more than the money to him. He brings in so much value. The level at which he connects with people, emotional level, spiritual level, professional level, you learn so much from him. It's amazing! I thank God I found him. I appreciate you so deeply Robert, much deeper than I can say." Omezikam Ugwa

"Robert is amazing, and we are honored to be working with him. Robert is not afraid to step out and try the new things and most importantly succeed while trying." Pasha Carter

"Robert has shaped me into who I am today. That says a lot. There are not that many people who can influence or impact you in really positive ways. Robert's different perspective in life is where he enjoys life. He has done it and grasps the concepts of enjoying life and understanding your why. Thank you for helping me in the past and helping me where I am at today." Jesse Perreault

It's great to have someone with so much knowledge and experience to guide and direct us in the right direction! Thanks so much, Robert Hollis!   Robert Dorsey

The value of what you have poured into me is immeasurable. Not only are you a blessing but I too find it a privilege to call you my dear friend. YOU absolutely ROCK!   Lori Anne Lady Boss Hayes

Robert, you are the most generous and humble person I know. Your friendship and mentorship have gone much further affecting my personal and spiritual life. Thank you for all you have done for me.   Bob Cline

Robert helped me figure out something that no one was able to help me figure out for years. Thank-you Robert. I'm so humbled, blessed and "SUPER" excited to have you coach me.   Curtis Phelan

MY I AM STATEMENTS

Robert Hollis Enthusiastic Entrepreneurial Evangelist

I am ...

*whole, perfect, strong, powerful, loving, *harmonious and happy!

*competent, capable, and worthy!

*surrounded by trusting and trustworthy friends!

*bringing value to everyone!

*a child of God and the universe he created!

*sorry, please forgive me, thank you and I love you!

*a success. I can be, do and have everything I want.

*bold, present, enthusiastic

*comfortable with riches and success.

*enthusiastically achieving my goals.

*I am creating success.

*willing to take well-thought-out risks to move toward success and riches

I am so Happy and Grateful NOW that _____ money comes to me in increasing quantities from multiple sources on a continuous basis!

I feel _____

*deeply and fully accepting of myself!

*safe and secure in my life!

*loved and deserving of love!

God's wealth is circulating in my life. His wealth flows to me in avalanches of abundance. Instantaneously all my needs, desires and goals are met because I am one with God, and God is everything!

Wouldn't it be cool if _____?

I can do _____

   * anything I put my mind to. I vividly picture what I want and resolutely move toward it. Prosperity is circulating in my life. Prosperity flows to me in avalanches of abundance. I deserve money and success.

My needs, desires, and goals are met instantaneously. I have unlimited self-confidence.

My life overflows with abundance, prosperity, riches, and success. Ideas are now coming to me that will help me achieve whatever I want in life. I immediately and enthusiastically act toward my goals.

My thoughts are powerful, and I effortlessly direct them toward what I want. I act with confidence to implement the creative ideas I am always receiving.

THE GOD MEMORANDUM

Excerpts from the <u>World's Greatest Miracle-</u> By Og Mandino

You are my finest creation. Therefore, I say unto you, count your blessings, and know that you already are my greatest creation. This is the first law you must obey to perform the greatest miracle in the world, the return of your humanity from living death...

Count your blessings... And the second law is like unto the first. Proclaim your rarity...

You alone persevered within the loving warmth of your mother's body, searching for your other half, a single cell from your mother so small that more than two million would be necessary to fill an acorn shell. Yet, despite impossible odds, in that vast ocean of darkness and disaster, you persevered, found that infinitesimal cell joined with it, and began a new life. Your life...

You! One of a kind, Rarest of the rare, A priceless treasure, possessed of qualities in mind and speech and movement and appearance and actions as no other who has ever lived, lives, or shall live...

Why have you valued yourself in pennies when you are worth a king's ransom? You are my greatest miracle... Count your blessings! Proclaim your rarity! Go another mile!...

I gave you the power to think.

I gave you the power to love.

I gave you the power to will.

I gave you the power to laugh.

I gave you the power to imagine.

I gave you the power to create.

I gave you the power to plan.

I gave you the power to speak.

I gave you the power to pray.

I gave you the power to heal.

I gave you ... the power to choose... What is past is past

Choose to love ... rather than hate.

Choose to laugh ... rather than cry.

Choose to create ... rather than destroy.

Choose to persevere ... rather than quit.

Choose to praise ... rather than gossip.

Choose to heal ... rather than wound.

Choose to give ... rather than steal.

Choose to act ... rather than procrastinate.

Choose to grow ... rather than rot.

Choose to pray ... rather than a curse.

Choose to live ... rather than die.

Remember, then, the four laws of happiness and success... Count your blessings, proclaim your rarity, go another mile, and use wisely your power of choice.

And one more to fulfill the other four, do all things with love ... love for yourself, love for all others, and love for me

COMING FALL OF 2018

FOREWORD BY ROBERT HOLLIS

ARE YOU STUCK?

Embracing Change By Releasing Your Potential

HELP

LAURIE MONSON

56163821R00104

Made in the USA
Columbia, SC
21 April 2019